THE INCOMPLETE GUIDE TO THE

WILDLIFE OF SAINT MARTIN

BY MARK YOKOYAMA

A view of Pointe des Froussards from Bell Hill with Rocher Marcel in the foreground. Scrubland near the coast gives way to dry tropical forest.

INTRODUCTION

As you may have guessed from the title, this field guide is not a comprehensive guide to the wildlife of St. Martin. Such a guide would be much longer and require significantly more expertise in a variety of areas. The species included are restricted primarily to those which I have personally seen and photographed. That said, this guide does include most of the species one is likely to see when visiting the island.

Certain taxa are covered briefly, and many species are omitted entirely. The content has been researched and written by an individual with no professional background in zoology. Should you find these omissions and shortcomings intolerable, I encourage you to find a different guide to the fauna of this island. This may be difficult, as I know of no such volume.

Conversely, certain areas are covered in significant de-

tail. This is particularly true of species and varieties that are endemic either to this island or restricted to the Lesser Antilles. I believe this to be a valuable approach to the wildlife of this island. For example, many bird species on the island are common throughout the Americas and information about them is readily available from a variety of sources. On the other hand, several of the lizard species here are limited to just a few small islands and have been the subject of far less study.

This volume concludes with some notes on conservation and descriptions of some representative natural habitats on the island.

I apologize in advance for any inaccuracies, and I hope that should this volume ever be reviewed by a professional these may be corrected in future editions. If you have obtained this guide in order to enrich your own explorations of this fine island, happy exploring!

ABOUT THE ISLAND

Saint Martin, also known as Sint Maarten, is one of the Leeward Islands of the Lesser Antilles and is located in the Northeast Caribbean, bordering the Atlantic Ocean. The Lesser Antilles are volcanic islands, formed where the Atlantic Plate is pushed beneath the Caribbean Plate. The island was formed about 20 million years ago, and subsequently submerged beneath the sea and was capped with limestone rock, which is now clearly visible in many parts of the island. It is significantly less mountainous than newer islands, such as nearby Saba, but does have a range of small mountains, the tallest being Pic Paradis at 424 meters.

Saint Martin is approximately 87 square kilometers in size and ownership is divided between France (Saint Martin) and the Netherlands Antilles (Sint Maarten), with France occupying the northern 60% of the island. The current population is around 80,000, with a majority living on the Dutch side. There are a few neighboring islets, primarily on the French side, the largest being Tintamarre and Ilet Pinel.

Like the other Lesser Antilles, Saint Martin was never connected to a continent. Subsequently, it has a relatively low diversity of native fauna, particularly those that cannot fly. During the colonial period most native habitats were destroyed for agriculture, including deforestation of the interior and the draining of mangrove wetlands. It is presumed that at least most of the current forests are secondary growth. The introduction of non-native animals, both accidental (rats, mice) and deliberate (livestock, mongoose) has also been implicated in the destruction of habitat and the extinction of native species. More recently, development for tourism has resulted in further habitat destruction and degradation of habitats such as the lagoon and the numerous salt ponds on the island.

There are a variety of habitats on the island. Without peaks high enough to support a cloud forest, the highlands are primarily tropical deciduous forest, where many trees lose leaves during the dry season. Dry scrubland also makes up a good deal of the interior of the island, particularly in areas that are used as pasture for goats or cattle. There are numerous salt ponds on the island, and most are ringed with mangrove wetlands. While there are dry gulches that may fill temporarily after strong rains, there are no permanent rivers or significant fresh water ponds. Beaches and rocky shorelines ring the island, and in areas that are not developed, littoral (seaside) forest or scrub can be found. There is a large, enclosed lagoon in the southwest part of the island. In the seas surrounding the island, a mix of sand, seagrass beds and coral reefs can be found.

Mangroves filled with roosting egrets surround the salt pond Étang de Cimetiere near Grand Case. Behind it, Smith Hill is covered with dry scrubland.

Highland forests can be quite dense, but gullies like this one on Hope Hill almost never have running water and are typically the easiest way to access the forests in areas where there are no trails.

A large cluster of bats (probably *Brachyphylla cavernarum cavernarum*) roosting in La Grotte de Puits de Terres Basses in the lowland area of the island. Hundreds of bats from several species of bat have been observed in this large cave.

MAMMALS

On Saint Martin, the only native mammals are bats, although dolphins and whales may be seen in the surrounding seas, either year-round or seasonally. The majority of mammals on the island are introduced species, including livestock, pets and pests.

In prehistoric times, there were at least two native rodents, the blunt-toothed giant hutia (*Amblyrhiza inundata*), which may have been as large as 200 kg, and a much smaller, semi-aquatic oryzomyine. While it is unclear if the giant hutia was present when the island was first colonized by the Arawaks (the first known human residents of the island), oryzomyine remains have been found at archaeological sites on the island.

BATS

There are thought to be eight species of bat (order Chi-roptera) currently on the island: the greater fishing bat (*Noctilio leporinus mastivus*), the insular long-tongued bat (*Monophyllus plethodon luciae*), the Antillean cave bat (*Brachyphylla cavernarum cavernarum*), the Lesser Antillean tree bat (*Ardops nichollsi montserratensis*), the Jamaican fruit-eating bat (*Artibeus jamaicensis jamaicensis*), the Lesser Antillean funnel-eared bat (*Natalus stramineus stramineus*), the Brazilian free-tailed bat (*Tadarida brasiliensis antillularum*) and Pallas' mastiff bat (*Molossus molossus molossus*). Bats may often be seen flying at night, and also roost in some buildings. There are also two caves on the island where several species are known to roost.

Due to the difficulty in identifying bats from photos (versus captured specimens), the identifications in this section are tentative. Some characteristics, such as color, size and presence of a noseleaf may be seen in photos. Others, like whether the tail extends beyond the tail membrane, may not be ascertained by photos alone.

A single bat, likely *Artibeus jamaicensis*, hangs from the ceiling of La Grotte de Puits de Terres Basses. The floor of the western chamber of the cave was covered in almond seeds and fruit pits.

Another likely *Artibeus jamaicensis*, found in a cave at the top of Billy Folly on the Dutch side of the island. These are thought to be the most common bats on the island.

A large mass of what are probably *Brachyphylla cavernarum cavernarum* in the eastern chamber of La Grotte de Puits. Although this chamber hosts multiple species, the floor was not covered with fruit pits.

This appears to be a *Brachyphylla cavernarum cavernarum* maternity colony in a recess in the ceiling of La Grotte de Puits. Larger adults are mixed with what appear to be juvenile bats.

This small group seems to include a mother and at least two young, one of which is clinging to the mother. The species seems to be *Artibeus jamaicensis*.

Bats in flight and roosting on the ceiling of La Grotte de Puits. In addition to smaller maternity colonies, large masses of bats, including dozens or hundreds pressed together, may be found.

INTRODUCED MAMMALS

Several species of mammal have been introduced to Saint Martin over the years. Black rats (*Rattus rattus*) and mice (*Mus musculus* and perhaps other species) have probably been here since the first European settlement of the island. I have noticed rats mostly in populated areas, and some particularly agile individuals can be seen performing tightrope antics on power cables at night. I have seen mice under a board in a field in La Savane, but I would guess they are quite widespread. I have also encountered mouse bones in bird pellets.

The small Asian mongoose (*Herpestes javanicus*) was introduced to Saint Martin in 1888, and is still found on the island. Presumably introduced to control snakes (although at the time of introduction there was likely only one, non-venomous species of snake), the mongoose has likely contributed to the decline of local reptile populations since its introduction.

This small, elongated varmint is usually gray-brown and I have only seen it briefly before it retreats into the woods or the shelter of a pile of brush or bramble, in which I would guess they have a burrow. I have seen it on Pic Paradis, and in dry forest areas near Grand Case and Anse Marcel.

The raccoon (*Procyon* sp.) is a mysterious resident of the island. First documented on the island in 1957, it has been seen sporadically since. I found one raccoon carcass in the valley leading to Bell Beach, which would suggest that this animal is still living on the island. The method, date and reason for their introduction is unknown, but it is generally assumed that they were introduced by man, as is the case on several nearby islands.

I have seen mongoose in both scrubland and densely forested areas on the island. They are wary of humans and tend to hide quickly. They are also curious and may return to investigate.

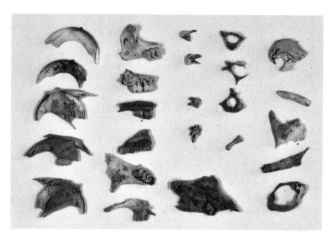

Rodent remains made up a large portion of some bird pellets I found.

Raccoon carcass found in Bell Valley. How can you tell it's a raccoon? In this case, I had also seen it a few weeks earlier when it was a little more recognizable.

OPPOSITE: A donkey photographed near Cul de Sac. A large group of donkeys is sometimes present here and they are quite friendly or at least optimistic about receiving handouts.

These goat kids were resting beneath a rocky overhang during an afternoon shower. While goats are often seen roaming freely over large areas of scrub and forest, the majority sport small plastic tags on their ears and return in the evenings for water and shelter.

LIVESTOCK AND PETS

Livestock on the island includes goats (*Capra aegagrus hircus*), cattle (*Bos primigenius*), horses (*Equus ferus caballus*), donkeys (*Equus africanus asinus*) and pigs (*Sus domestica*), while cats (*Felis catus*) and dogs (*Canis lupus familiaris*) are kept as pets. A few goats, cats and dogs are feral, but most have human owners.

Goats are the most common mammalian livestock on Saint Martin and they can be seen roaming the hills, wandering down roadsides and tied in front yards. Although many goats may seem to be wild when out in the scrub, most are tagged on the ear and return to shelters for water daily. With voracious appetites, goats transform the landscape significantly. The fence lines demarcating goat pasture often also mark a stark division between closely-cropped grass and diverse scrubland.

By comparison, cattle seem to be much more selective in their eating habits and areas used for cattle pasture may retain a more natural appearance. Like most goats, cattle are typically left to roam large areas of hillside during the day, but return for water and shelter in the evening. In late afternoon, they may be heard calling loudly to other members of their herd.

Horses and donkeys are less common and typically corralled, rather than free ranging. I have seen pigs in and around a series of pens beside Étang Guichard near Friars' Bay, and in Bell Valley, but they seem to make up a very small proportion of the livestock on the island.

Cats and dogs, while mostly pets, may also wander free as scavengers, particularly around towns, cities and developed beaches. I did once see a feral cat on the side of Bell Hill that I believe was living entirely in the wild. Having seen this only once in my many travels, I would guess this situation is relatively uncommon.

This small mule was tied up near a path in Colombier, and though somewhat frightened, was quite friendly.

Cattle roam freely in many parts of the island, like this one in the abandoned, hurricane-damaged development near Happy Bay. Members of this herd are also frequently seen on the beach.

There are a number of pig enclosures along the shore of Étang Guichard near Friars' Bay. While some pigs may be seen roaming freely in that area, there does not seem to be a wild population.

Dog and cat overpopulation is a serious problem on the island. The majority live in developed areas and scavenge refuse, which probably lessens their impact on more natural environments.

THE INCOMPLETE GUIDE TO THE WILDLIFE OF SAINT MARTIN   9

The common ground dove (*Columbigallina passerina nigrirostris*) is much smaller than the other doves on the island and unlike some of the other doves it is less common in urban environments, preferring fields and scrubland.

BIRDS

Over 100 species of birds have been observed on Saint Martin, including approximately 40 breeding residents. The remainder are either seasonally migrant visitors or the occasional vagrant. Saint Martin has no endemic species of bird, but it does have two species and six subspecies that are endemic to the Lesser Antilles.

The relative paucity of species is attributed to the small size of the island, extensive habitat destruction and, for some species, hunting. Hurricanes may also have a severe impact, particularly on species that are already stressed by human activity.

This section of the guide is not comprehensive, but does include the majority of commonly seen birds and all those which are endemic to this part of the Caribbean. The species that follow are grouped by type, which often serves as an indication of where they are most com-

monly found, from the seabirds patrolling the offshore waters to waterfowl in the salt ponds and the terrestrial species occupying a variety of inland habitats.

The osprey (*Pandion haliaetus*) is one of many non-breeding species which may be seen either seasonally or only very rarely. These visitors make up the majority of bird species documented on the island.

SEABIRDS

Seabirds include a variety of birds from several orders that are adapted to life at sea. They may either be coastal, or spend much of their time on the open ocean. Their primary diet consists of fish and other marine life. The majority of seabirds nest in colonies, and suitable nesting sites are crucial to their survival.

The high level of human activity and development, coupled with egg-eating predators such as the rat and mongoose, have resulted in decreased seabird nesting activity on St. Martin. A number of small offshore islets, however, remain important nesting sites for many seabirds.

These islets include Creole Rock, Caye Chateau, Pelican Key, Molly Beday and Hen and Chickens, all of which are known nesting sites for various species of seabird. For the most part, these are very small rocky formations with little vegetation. Larger satellite islands, such as Tintamarre, Pinel and Caye Verte also serve as nesting sites, but unfortunately are populated by rats. On the mainland, relatively isolated seaside cliffs serve as nesting sites for some species like the tropicbirds.

Although nesting populations of most seabirds have declined in St. Martin as they have in the rest of the world, the presence of many active nesting sites, particularly on isolated islets, has given some researchers reason to consider it one of the more important seabird nesting sites in the Caribbean.

An immature brown booby in flight. When it matures, the light brown area on the underside of the body and wings will turn white, while the darker brown areas will remain dark brown.

This juvenile brown booby has eaten a needle-nosed fish that it is unable to swallow. It was easily approached because its large meal made it unable or unwilling to fly.

BROWN BOOBY (*Sula leucogaster*)

The brown booby is a large seabird that may nest on isolated islets in the area. It is a member of the gannet family (Sulidae). They may be seen around the island throughout the year, but are generally less common than the magnificent frigatebird and brown pelican. Most often, they are seen fishing in waters near the coast or roosting along rocky shorelines.

Building exposed nests on the ground, this species is highly vulnerable to predation by introduced species such as the rat.

Small offshore rocks and islets like Rocher Creole (Creole Rock) are relatively free from human disturbance and introduced predators, making them important nesting areas for seabirds.

BROWN PELICAN (*Pelecanus occidentalis occidentalis*)

The brown pelican is easily identified by its ungainly but endearing shape. The largest seabird on the island, it is typically seen fishing near shore alone. There is known to be a nesting colony on the appropriately-named Pelican Key on the Dutch side of the island. Other nesting colonies have also been noted on Green Cay on the French side, and Molly Beday. The brown pelican is found on both coasts in North and South America, but the subspecies *occidentalis* is limited to the Caribbean.

In this pair of flying pelicans the all-brown juvenile is above the adult. Although often seen alone or in pairs, on occasion groups of a dozen or more may be seen fishing together.

Adult brown pelicans have a white head and neck, although the top of the head may be yellowish or tan. Between fishing trips, they roost on rocks to dry their wings.

In the trees near Happy Bay large groups of pelicans roost in the evening. The friend who pointed this out to me had first discovered this roosting area decades ago.

This brown pelican is diving for fish. Unlike some seabirds, they dive directly into the water rather than trying to catch fish at the surface.

The brown pelican is a strong flyer, although take-off from the water is difficult. They must first expel any water from their gullet, while retaining any fish they have caught. They then take flight with much energetic flapping.

A large group of laughing gulls searches for food in a tidal flat near Grande Caye. Even larger groups may be seen scavenging at the nearby dump.

The sandwich tern is a summer visitor to the island and can be identified by its long, white-tipped, black bill.

The laughing gull could be mistaken for a similarly-colored tern, but the whole head is black, not just the crown, and the back is generally a darker gray.

The beak of the royal tern is entirely orange yellow, but it is otherwise quite similar to several other tern species seen on the island.

LAUGHING GULL (*Larus atricilla*)

The laughing gull is very common during the summer months, when it nests on Pelican Key and probably in other locations. Large flocks can be seen in tidal areas and scavenging near popular beaches. Like many gulls, juveniles are gray in color and lack the distinctive markings of the adult. During the winter months they are much less common on the island.

In addition to coastal areas, these gulls may be seen at the various salt ponds as well as inland scavenging locations such as the local dump. A relatively poor hunter, they may be seen landing on or near pelicans in an attempt to steal food from their beaks.

SANDWICH TERN (*Sterna sandwicensis*) AND ROYAL TERN (*Sterna maxima*)

There are a number of tern (family Sternidae) species seen on the island, including several which breed here. Most are predominantly white with some dark markings and all are superb, graceful fliers. The breeding species include the sooty tern (*Sterna fuscata*), least tern (*Sternula antillarum antillarum*), roseate tern (*Sterna dougallii*), bridled tern (*Sterna anaethetus*) and royal tern. The common tern (*Sterna hirundo*) and sandwich tern are seasonal migrants that do not breed here.

A female (black head) and juvenile (white head) engage in aerial acrobatics near the beach at Grande Caye. Their distinctive forked tails are clearly visible.

Tropicbirds may easily be distinguished by their very long tail feathers, which may actually be longer than their body.

The male magnificent frigatebird has a bright red, inflatable throat pouch that is used in courtship. Clearly visible in this photo, but not totally inflated, it is normally only slightly visible, if at all.

It is highly likely that tropicbirds are nesting in the relatively inaccessible seaside cliffs of Tintamarre, St. Martin's largest satellite island.

MAGNIFICENT FRIGATEBIRD (*Fregata magnificens*)

The magnificent frigatebird is the second-largest seabird on the island and is most frequently seen circling high over the water. Often large groups circle near choice locations, and they may be seen stealing food from smaller birds, particularly the laughing gull.

These birds are seen year-round, and may breed in mangrove woodlands on the island, but no nesting colonies are currently identified. In fact, there are few known nesting sites in the Caribbean, perhaps due to the practice of draining and clearing mangrove wetlands for development. Locally, this bird is often referred to as the scissorsbird or man o'war.

RED-BILLED TROPICBIRD (*Phaeton aethereus mesonauta*)

I most frequently see this bird near the offshore island of Tintamarre, where I believe it nests. Other possible nesting locations include seaside cliffs on the main island, as well as uninhabited offshore rocks like Creole Rock and Molly Beday. The white-tailed tropicbird (*Phaethon lepturus*) is very similar in appearance and is also known to nest in St. Martin.

EGRETS AND HERONS

The family Ardeidae includes egrets and herons, elongated, carnivorous wading birds that often live and feed in wetland areas. Most species are at least somewhat migratory, and the population of several species on St. Martin has considerable seasonal variation.

The best place to observe these birds is in and around the many salt ponds and mangrove woodlands on the island. In addition to the species featured here, the great blue heron (*Ardea herodias*) is at least an occasional visitor to the island.

Bright yellow feet at the end of black legs are indicative of this egret. The wispy tail feathers can also be seen in this photo.

A yellow bill, black legs and large size identify the great egret. The great blue heron (*Ardea heriodias*) in its white phase is similar, but with gray legs and red-brown thigh plumage, and I have not seen it on the island in that color.

SNOWY EGRET (*Egretta thula*)

The snowy egret is a smallish, white egret with whispy plumage on its head and tail. It can be identified by its black (adult) or yellow and black (immature) legs with yellow feet and black bill. It primarily frequents salt pond and mangrove wetlands. Although it is not thought to breed on most of the Lesser Antilles, it does breed on St. Martin.

GREAT EGRET (*Egretta gularis*)

The great egret is quite large and is found in the various salt ponds on the island where it fishes. In the evening, I have seen them calling loudly from hillsides near salt ponds. This species typically breeds in trees near wetlands, making the local mangrove forests a potential breeding location, although it is unclear if breeds on the island.

I have seen the closely-related great blue heron (*Ardea herodias*) on one occasion, but in the dark color phase which could not be mistaken for the great egret.

Breeding adults sport patches of orangish-tan on their head, chest and backs. Non-breeding adults are entirely white. They can be distinguished from other egrets and herons by their yellow legs.

The green heron is not actually green. It is dark above with brown sides and has yellow legs. There is a distinctive yellow-green stripe from the eye to the beak and a brown and white streaked neck and chest.

Cattle egrets are generally gregarious and are frequently seen in fields. The similarly colored snowy egret is typically seen alone.

Juvenile green herons have a streaked neck and breast. The top of the head is not as dark, nor is the back.

CATTLE EGRET (*Bubulcus ibis*)

The cattle egret is an exceedingly common year-round resident of the island. As its name indicates, it is often seen in pastures near cattle, feeding on insects and other small animals that are disturbed by the cattle. Studies have shown that it is several times more successful at hunting when near a large animal than it is when alone.

In the evening, cattle egrets roost primarily in mangroves, often in large groups of a dozen or more individuals. They also breed in colonies in wetland areas, making nests in mangrove trees.

GREEN HERON (*Butorides virescens*)

The green heron is a small, nocturnal heron that breeds on St. Martin. Like other herons, it is typically seen near salt ponds and mangrove wetlands, but it also prowls near the beach at night.

The diet of the green heron is primarily small fish, frogs and invertebrates. They are known to drop insects or other small objects into the water to attract fish. This opportunistic feeder is also thought to eat bird eggs, including those of the bananaquit, giving it a bad reputation on the island. This species breeds on Saint Martin, primarily in mangrove wetlands. Locally it is referred to as the night heron or tick picker.

The yellow-crowned night heron has a large red eye and a thick bill. It has a yellow-tan crown that extends behind its head and a white band below the eye.

Immature yellow-crowned night herons are a mottled brown color, but can easily be identified by their stocky build and thick beak.

YELLOW-CROWNED NIGHT HER-ON (*Nyctanassa violacea*)

The yellow-crowned night heron is large and stocky, and can be seen occasionally during the day, although it is also primarily nocturnal. It feeds primarily on fish, frogs and invertebrates.

This species tends to breed in colonies, making nests in trees. There is one such colony in the forested northeastern point of Pinel Islet just off the coast of Saint Martin.

WETLAND BIRD WATCHING

The wetland areas of St. Martin are probably the most rewarding locations for bird watching. One can naturally expect to see waterfowl, waders and egrets in and around the salt ponds, but a variety of other species are quite common there as well.

The close proximity to the ocean often draws seabirds to the salt ponds, particularly laughing gulls and brown pelicans. The nearby mangrove forests are often home to a variety of passerines including the yellow warbler, carib grackle and gray kingbird.

The presence of chicks from breeding species, like the common moorhen, is a special treat when bird watching in the mangroves and ponds during summer and fall.

A great egret and two cattle egrets roosting in a mangrove tree in the early evening.

WADING BIRDS

There is a large variety of wading birds, including species that are primarily found on the beach and in rocky tidal zones, as well as those who prefer salt ponds, mud flats and mangrove wetlands. Many of these species are non-breeding migrants that are only found during certain times of year, other species may reside here year-round and breed on the island. On the island, wading birds in general are typically referred to as pond birds.

The black-necked stilt (*Himantopus mexicanus*) is a tall salt pond wader with pink legs, a long black bill and distinct black and white markings. When approached, they make continuous warning calls.

The ruddy turnstone (*Arenaria interpres*) is a small wader sometimes seen on beaches or rocky shores. It can be identified by its facial markings and red legs.

The willet (*Catoptrophorus semipalmatus*) is gray brown and can be identified by its thick bill and gray legs.

The American oystercatcher (*Haematopus palliatus*) is a large wading bird seen in tidal areas. It is easily identified by its long, thick, red bill, black head and neck and pink legs.

The greater yellowlegs (*Tringa melanoleuca*) has yellow legs, of course. It also is larger and has a longer bill than the lesser yellowlegs (*T. flavipes*). Both may be seen in wetlands from August to October.

The least sandpiper (*Calidris minutilla*) is the smallest sandpiper on the island, and can be distinguished from its very similar cousins by its bright yellow legs.

The adult killdeer has two black bands on its breast and is larger than the various plovers that may be seen on the island. It is quite similar to its relatives in general coloration and facial markings.

The semipalmated sandpiper (*Calidris pusilla*) is often seen in flocks near ponds from August through October. A similar species, the western sandpiper (*C. mauri*), has a longer bill and is slightly larger, but otherwise looks very similar.

A killdeer chick sports a dark headband and tries to hide when approached.

KILLDEER (*Charadrius vociferus*)

The killdeer is a common breeding resident of the island that is found in wet fields, often near puddles or other wet damp areas. They nest on the ground, and adults often pretend to be injured while calling loudly in order to attract attention and lure potential predators away from their nest. When approached, chicks typically attempt to flee on foot. If that fails, they hide, often very poorly.

The killdeer is a type of plover, and is related to the wading birds found on the island, although it generally is found in open fields rather than wetlands.

The semipalmated plover (*Charadrius semipalmatus*) is the only common plover on the island and is seen here in non-breeding coloration. Wilson's plover (*C. wilsonia*) and the snowy plover (*C. alexandrinus*) may also be occasional residents or visitors.

WATERFOWL

The waterfowl of St. Martin includes a variety of ducks as well as several related species. While some nest locally, particularly during the summer months, others are migrants who are merely passing through. The preservation of the many salt ponds on the island is crucial to the continued presence of these species. Ducks and geese are members of the family Anatidae, while the coots and the moorhen are members of the family Rallidae, which also includes rails.

The muscovy duck (*Cairina moschata*) is a common domestic species on the island. They are very large, usually black and white in color and have warty, red faces.

The male ruddy duck has a distinctive blue bill, particularly during the breeding season. There is also a distinct depression on the back of the head.

A white-cheeked pintail takes flight from a field bordering a salt pond. The white cheek and red area of the bill make this species easy to identify, even from a distance.

The female ruddy duck is fairly nondescript, but has a defined brown line through the light patch on its cheek. It is, of course, much easier to identify when traveling with its mate.

WHITE-CHEEKED PINTAIL (*Anas bahamensis*)

This species is considered rare in the Lesser Antilles, but may be relatively more common in St. Martin due to the presence of a large number of salt ponds.

Also known as the Bahama pintail, these ducks may be seen in pairs or in larger groups, primarily in the salt ponds of the island. The sexes are quite similar in appearance. They feed on plant matter and small animals by dabbling on the surface.

RUDDY DUCK (*Oxyura jamaicensis*)

The ruddy duck is another species thought to be rare in the Lesser Antilles, but pairs are not difficult to find in St. Martin. It seems probable that many waterfowl are generally more common here than on neighboring islands due to the large number of salt ponds.

The ruddy duck may also be seen in mixed groups with the white-cheeked pintail, sometimes numbering a dozen or more. They dive frequently when feeding, and their diet consists of both plant material and various invertebrates.

Both sexes of the common moorhen are similar in appearance and easily identified by their yellow-tipped red beak, which extends up to the forehead.

The American coot can be identified by the red knobs at the top of the frontal shield of the bill. It is otherwise very similar to the Caribbean coot.

A pair of common moorhens building their nest in the canal that seasonally connects the Grand Case airport salt pond to the ocean.

The Caribbean coot has a white shield extending from the bill to the crown of the head and does not have red knobs at the top. From a distance, the two species may be impossible to tell apart.

ANTILLEAN COMMON MOORHEN (*Gallinula chloropus cerceris*)

This common, year-round resident is locally called the water chicken because of its chicken-like, unwebbed feet. It is seen in and around the salt ponds, nesting in the summer in low hanging mangrove branches on the water. Moorhen chicks are fuzzy and black with red beaks and a slightly balding head. Immature fledglings are typically brown with a dark beak.

Common moorhens, more than other waterfowl, seem to be quite comfortable around humans. They are commonly seen feeding and even nesting near human habitations and well-trafficked areas.

AMERICAN COOT (*Fulica americana*) AND CARIBBEAN COOT (*Fulica caribaea*)

These two coots are both found on the island, typically during the summer months. It is likely that they breed in the wetlands near salt ponds. Very similar in appearance, the Caribbean coot's white bill extends into a frontal shield to the top of its head and lacks red knobs at the top. Coot chicks are similar to those of the common moorhen, dark and baldish, but with additional orange plumes around the neck. Immature fledglings are gray in color, with a lighter underside.

TERRESTRIAL BIRDS

Although the diversity of terrestrial birds on St. Martin is not particularly great, there are representatives of at least four orders. There are no island endemics, but two species and six subspecies are endemic to the Lesser Antilles as a whole, all of which are featured in this section. There are a number of nesting species, as well as migrant and vagrant visitors that appear seasonally.

Habitat loss and introduced predators have reduced overall bird populations on the island. Hurricanes temporarily reduce bird populations by disrupting food supplies and destroying nests. The impact of natural disasters is exacerbated by human-caused stresses, making it more difficult for populations to survive and recover.

The male American kestrel has a black spots on the breast, rather than brown streaks like the female. There are several distinct subspecies present in the Caribbean.

The male American kestrel has blue-gray wings and crown, with a reddish-brown back. Two large black spots can also be seen on the back of the head.

This female American kestrel scans the Grand Case cemetery for potential prey from a perch high on a nearby palm tree. These small birds of prey can be found in a variety of habitats in all parts of the island.

AMERICAN KESTREL (*Falco sparverius caribaearum*)

The American kestrel is a small falcon that is common throughout much of the Americas. It is probably the only raptor breeding on the island, and definitely the most commonly seen.

Also known as the sparrow hawk, and locally as the killy-killy, these birds may be identified by their distinctive facial markings. The sexes are somewhat different in coloration. Both are predominantly orange-brown on their backs, but the male has blue-gray wings. The breast of the female is off-white with tan streaks, while that of the male is typically orangish-tan with dark spots.

HUMMINGBIRDS

From the family Trochilidae, hummingbirds are typically very small, and have amazing flying abilities, including the ability to hover and fly backwards.

There are probably only two species of hummingbird on the island. Both species are endemic to the Lesser Antilles.

A third species that might be present is the purple-throated carib (*Eulampis jugularis*). Although this hummingbird is found on nearby islands, it seems to prefer higher elevations than St. Martin has to offer.

The green-throated carib is an iridescent green in the right light, but also may appear mostly black. It is larger than the Antillean crested hummingbird, with a longer, curved bill. (Photo by M.P.)

This Antillean crested hummingbird was feeding from flowers just after a hurricane passed. During this time it was easier to see hummingbirds at the few intact flowers in the area.

ANTILLEAN CRESTED HUMMING-BIRD (*Orthorhyncus cristatus exilios*)

The Antillean crested hummingbird is subspecifically endemic to the Lesser Antilles and is generally quite common. It can be identified by the green crest and straight bill and is often seen feeding from flowers in gardens. This species is much smaller than the green-throated carib.

It is thought that hurricanes have a serious impact on hummingbird populations by causing nectar shortages, which are serious for birds with such a high metabolism.

GREEN-THROATED CARIB (*Sericotes holosericeus holocereus*)

The green-throated carib may appear black in flight, but has iridescent green plumage on the throat and head. It can be distinguished from the Antillean crested hummingbird by its lack of a crest as well as its longer, curved beak.

The purple-throated carib (*Eulampis jugularis*), if it is present on the island, is quite similar in appearance, but can be distinguished by its purple throat.

DOVES AND PIGEONS

The doves and pigeons, from the family Columbidae, include some of the most common, highly-visible birds on the island. Although many were heavily hunted, a decline in hunting has caused several species to rebound in population. Many of these birds are quite common in urban areas, particularly the zenaida and Eurasian collared doves.

In addition to the doves featured here, the rock dove (*Columba livia*) is an introduced species that may be found in towns, particularly Marigot. It is easily recognized as this species is what many North Americans and Europeans simply refer to as pigeons.

The zenaida dove can easily be identified by its orangish-brown color, black spots and white wing band. It also has a black crescent mark on its neck.

The Eurasian collared dove is similar in size to the zenaida dove, but is a light gray-brown with a distinct black and white collar around the back of its neck.

This individual was foraging on the ground when I approached, and adopted a strange stance, perhaps in an attempt to camouflage itself.

EURASIAN COLLARED DOVE (*Streptopelia decaocto*)

The Eurasian collared dove is an introduced species that has been expanding its range in the Caribbean. It currently seems less common on St. Martin than the similarly-sized zenaida dove, but it is entirely possible this balance will shift in the coming years. It seems to prefer developed areas. It can easily be identified by its light-gray coloration and distinct black and white collar. Locally they are also known as barbie doves.

ZENAIDA DOVE (*Zenaida aurita aurita*)

The zenaida dove is quite common on St. Martin, living primarily in open areas such as fields, roadsides and towns. They are also sometimes found inside my apartment. On one occasion I saw two individuals that seemed to be fighting, both employing a strange stance with one wing raised.

The subspecies *aurita* is endemic to the Lesser Antilles. The white tips of the secondary wing feathers distinguish this species from the eared dove and mourning dove. These similar species are not known on St. Martin, but do have expanding ranges in the Caribbean.

Common ground doves are indeed usually seen foraging on the ground, but will also roost in trees. I have often seen them in pairs or small groups.

The bright red wing feathers of the common ground dove are seen during flight. I have also witnessed doves spreading their wings while on the ground, perhaps as part of a courtship ritual.

The long, scaly-looking neck and red area around the eye make this relatively uncommon pigeon easy to identify, even from a distance.

COMMON GROUND DOVE (*Columbigallina passerina nigrirostris*)

The common ground dove is about half the size of the zenaida and Eurasian collared doves, and is found primarily in open areas away from human development. From a distance they appear to be a nondescript gray-brown, but in flight they reveal bright, brick red wing feathers. When seen up close, their head has a wonderful pearly sheen.

The subspecies *nigrirostris* is endemic to the Lesser Antilles, and it thankfully seems quite common on the island today.

SCALY-NAPED PIGEON (*Columba squamosa*)

One of several species that was hunted to near extinction on the island, this bird may be seen occasionally, primarily in remote areas. It is easily identified by its long neck and red patch around the eye. The neck feathers, which are a reflective red in the right light, have a scaly appearance which gives this bird its name.

This bird is endemic to the Caribbean, ranging from Cuba to the various offshore islands of Venezuela. On Saint Martin, it is often referred to as the copper neck or blue pigeon. It typically travels in pairs, while groups of four are usually a couple with their children.

PERCHING BIRDS

The order Passeriformes includes more than half of all bird species and the majority of perching birds on the island. Generally fairly small, these birds are quite diverse, and include seed-eaters, insectivores and nectar-drinkers that inhabit virtually every habitat on the island.

Also included in this section is one species of cuckoo, from the order Cuculiformes. The cuckoos are closely related to the passerines. Not pictured here is the barn swallow (*Hirundo rustica*), which is seasonally quite common and may be seen flying near the coast, salt ponds and other areas. It is quite small, has a forked tail and is an agile flyer.

The low, shrubby forest on Pinel island is home to many bananaquits, who also frequent the restaurant bars on the islet to drink simple syrup from unattended bottles.

This yellow warbler was seen in a mixed area of acacia bordering a mangrove woodland.

These bananaquit are enjoying sugar from a bird feeder. Their natural food is plant nectar, but their opportunistic feeding habits likely contribute immensely to their success on the island.

YELLOW WARBLER (*Dendroica petechia bartholemica*)

Another subspecies endemic to the northern Lesser Antilles, the yellow warbler, locally known as the gold-finch, does not seem very common on the island and is probably restricted to relatively small areas of scrubland and mangrove forest. The individuals I observed were actually seen at the border between these two habitats. They seemed to spend most of their time hopping from branch to branch inside the crowns of acacias and other trees.

This small bird is yellow with brown streaks on its breast. Immature birds and non-breeding females are generally brown with a faint cast of yellow.

BANANAQUIT (*Coereba flaveola bartholemica*)

This subspecies of bananaquit is named after nearby St. Barths and is found only in the northern Lesser Antilles. It is quite common near human habitation and is also called the sucriere or sugar bird due to its love of sugar. It may also be referred to as the yellow breast.

The taxonomy of the bananaquit is uncertain. It is tentatively placed in the family Thraupidae along with the finches of the Galapagos and grassquits, pending more certain classification. In 2010, the International Ornithological Congress also suggested splitting the varieties into three distinct species.

The male black-faced grassquit can be identified by its dark face and chest.

The male is easily identified by its coloration, which is predominantly black with reddish brown patches.

The female and immature black-faced grassquit are brown with no noticeable markings, although a bit of pink skin is usually visible at the base of the beak.

The female is quite difficult to distinguish from the female black-faced grassquit which is also present on the island. Some individuals may have orangish patches around the tail.

BLACK-FACED GRASSQUIT (*Tiaris bicolor*)

This small bird is generally common in the Caribbean and can often be seen in scrubland, open fields and near habitations. While the male is fairly easy to identify, the female may be difficult or impossible to distinguish from the female Lesser Antillean bullfinch.

Primarily a seed eater, it is a tanager, and is thought to be closely related to the finches of the Galapagos that were originally collected by Charles Darwin and were an important inspiration for his theory of evolution by means of natural selection. Along with the Lesser Antillean bullfinch, it is locally known as the chi-chi or sparrow.

LESSER ANTILLEAN BULLFINCH (*Loxigilla noctis ridgewayi*)

The Lesser Antillean bullfinch is another variety that is subspecifically endemic to the northern Lesser Antilles and is primarily seen in open scrubland and near habitations. The male is black with reddish patches on the neck, above the eye and around the butt. The female is a nondescript brown and may easily be mistaken for the female black-faced grassquit (*Tiaris bicolor*).

The name bullfinch comes from a resemblance to the European bullfinches, but currently these birds are believed to be part of the tanager family (Emberizidae). Locally, it may be referred to as the chi-chi or sparrow.

The male carib grackle is a shiny black, with bright eyes. They are slightly smaller than the pearly-eyed thrasher and slightly larger than the gray kingbird.

A pearly-eyed thrasher stares back in disdain after I interrupted its attack on a giant centipede.

The female carib grackle is slightly smaller and similar in shape to the male, but is brown with a lighter underside. Juveniles resemble the female, but have dark brown eyes.

The lighter-colored, longer beak helps distinguish this species from the smaller scaly-breasted thrasher (*Allenia fusca*), which I have not seen here, but does live on some nearby islands.

CARIB GRACKLE (*Quiscalus lugubris guadeloupensis*)

This bird is endemic to the Lesser Antilles at the subspecies level, and has only been reported on St. Martin since the 1970s. Males are all black and look a bit like a small crow, but have bright yellow eyes. Females are brown and relatively nondescript.

When courting, males have a song and dance routine that involves fluffing out their feathers and spreading their wings and tail while calling. They don't seem particularly common in most areas, but are very common near Mullet Bay and perhaps other preferred locations.

PEARLY-EYED THRASHER (*Margarops fuscatus*)

This thrasher is relatively common on the island and can often be seen in towns. It has a brown upper side and a white underside streaked with brown. The bill is long and yellow and the eye is a striking pearly white color. I have seen this bird carefully attacking a giant centipede (*Scolopendra* sp.), repeatedly jabbing it and then quickly jumping into the air to avoid being bitten.

The call of this bird often resembles the slide whistle part from Deee-lite's *Groove Is in the Heart*, but faster. The local name for this bird is thrush, pronounced trush.

In addition to scrubland areas, the gray kingbird may be seen around human habitation. It is one of the more common birds on the island.

The distinctive beak and dark, Zorro-style mask are clear markers of this species. The yellow underparts are not visible in this photo.

This gray kingbird was seen on its nest high in a tree at the edge of a scrubland area. I have also noticed nests atop telephone poles.

This individual seemed to be quite curious about me. Although it moved several times while I was watching it, it did not fly away. Having not seen it before, I was quite curious about it as well.

GRAY KINGBIRD (*Tyrannus dominicensis*)

The gray kingbird is a tyrant flycatcher and is quite common on the island. It can be seen both in scrubland and in towns and is identified by its gray head, gray-brown upper side and pale gray underside. Upon close inspection, small "whiskers" may be seen at the base of its bill. A orange stripe down the crown of the head may be present, but usually is not visible. Although there are several similar species in the Caribbean, none of them live on St. Martin. This bird is known locally as the chincherry.

MANGROVE CUCKOO (*Coccyzus minor*)

More than any other bird on the island, the mangrove cuckoo seemed quite curious about me. It is fairly large bird with some similarities to the gray kingbird. It has dirty yellow on the underside, primarily near the legs, resembling the northern variant of this species (the southern variant is yellow-orange on the underside from the neck to the tail). Other identifying features include a dark patch from the beak through the eye, and a beak that is black on top and yellow below. The tail feathers are black with white tips, giving the tail a black and white barred appearance. It frequents scrubland and mangrove woodlands.

This Anguilla bank anole (*Anolis gingivinus*) was photographed in the branches of a sea grape tree on the beach in Grand Case, a typical habitat for this very common species. *Anolis* is the most diverse genus of lizards in the Caribbean and in the world.

REPTILES

The reptiles on Saint Martin could be grouped into several categories: common and frequently seen, common but rarely seen, recently introduced, and probably extinct. More scientifically, including species that are possibly extinct here, there are eleven species of lizard, two snakes and one tortoise. This guide covers the ten species that I have seen and photographed.

The turnip-tailed gecko (*Thecadactylus rapicauda*) is cited in some literature as present on Saint Martin, although I have not seen it. It can be distinguished from the house gecko by its bulbous tail. The two-striped mabuya (*Mabuya bistriata*) is a skink that is cited as probably exterminated on the island. It is somewhat similar in appearance to *Amieva plei*, although it is shinier, moves in a smoother fashion and does not get as large.

The Lesser Antillean iguana (*Iguana delicatissima*) has been cited as probably exterminated from the island, although small populations still exist on other nearby islands. It is smaller than the common iguana (*Iguana iguana*), and lacks the large subtympanic scale present in that species. I have heard that some individuals may have been reintroduced, although interbreeding with the more common Iguana iguana makes it relatively unlikely that pure stock would remain on the island for very long.

The Leeward Island racer (*Alsophis rijersmai*), the only native snake on the island, is at best very rare. In fact, as early as the 1950s it was though to be eradicated, but specimens were seen in the 1990s. Apparently it is relatively common on Anguilla and St. Barths where there are no mongoose populations.

SEA TURTLES

In addition to the terrestrial reptile species covered in this volume, four species of sea turtle are known to live in the seas surrounding the island: the green turtle (*Chelonia midas*), hawksbill (*Erytmochelys imbricata*), loggerhead (*Caretta caretta*) and leatherback (*Dermochelys coriacea*). Only the hawksbill and green turtles are regularly seen when diving or snorkeling, as the loggerhead and leatherback primarily live in the open ocean rather than reefs or sea grass beds. Hawksbill, green and leatherback turtles all nest on the island and nearby islets. Although less common than in the past, tracks and nests can be seen from April through November, particularly on more secluded beaches.

Hawksbill turtles are frequently seen by divers and snorkelers on the reefs where they feed. Green turtles are also a relatively common sight, particularly in sea grass beds.

Tracks from a leatherback turtle show her ascent up the beach to find a suitable nesting site. Many attempted nests are aborted, often due to the presence of dogs.

ANOLES AND EVOLUTION

Anoles are a diverse group of lizards with over 400 known species worldwide. These small, primarily insectivorous lizards are related to iguanas and are often seen in trees or other elevated perches. They have the ability to change their color significantly, both for camouflage and for communication. They have a large dewlap, which is a flap of skin beneath the neck, that they are able to expand and retract to intimidate predators or rivals or to attract a mate.

Caribbean anoles have been the focus of much attention as an outstanding example of adaptive radiation, an evolutionary phenomenon where a species finding many unfilled niches evolves into multiple species uniquely adapted to fill these niches. In the case of anoles in the Caribbean, they first began colonizing the islands from South America about 40 million years ago. Today there are over 130 species of in the Caribbean alone.

Adapting to similar ecological niches on multiple islands resulted in the evolution of analogous species on different islands. While some of the Greater Antilles have dozens of species, in the Lesser Antilles the majority of islands have only one or two. Saint Martin features two species, and like nearby islands with two species, they differ in size and their preferred habitat. These differences allow them to coexist while competing less with each other for available food and space.

Early taxonomical efforts in this region were hampered by an overreliance on museum specimens. In a preface to a proposed reclassification done by Garth Underwood in the late 1950s, Ernest Williams remarked: "*Anolis* must be known intimately - anatomically, ecologically, ethologically - in all its relationships within and between species, if the many puzzles the genus poses are to be solved." Even today this work continues. One interesting approach involves the introduction of foreign species into controlled areas to observe the interaction and competition between species.

Anolis gingivinus displaying a fairly typical brown coloration with clearly visible dorsal band and white stripes on the sides. The dorsal band may be considerably less obvious in many individuals. Locally this species is often referred to as the tree lizard or fence lizard.

ANGUILLA BANK ANOLE (*Anolis gingivinus*)

Exceedingly common on St. Martin, Anguilla and St. Barths, this is one of many species historically considered part of the *bimaculatus* group of anoles found in the northern Lesser Antilles through Dominica and shares some characteristics with anoles of the Greater Antilles. Recent genetic analysis of these species indicates that the relationships between these species are more complicated than expected, and that *A. gingivinus* is a sister species to *A. bimaculatus*, which is found in St. Eustatius, St. Kitts and Nevis.

The Anguilla bank anole is the larger of the two anole species present on St. Martin and may be up to seven centimeters in snout-to-vent length (SVL), which basically means not counting the tail. It generally prefers sunny, elevated perches, and is often seen on tree trunks or branches. It has white bands on either side of the belly and an irregular band across the top, although the dorsal band may be obscured by spots or mottling, particularly in males. The coloration varies from light tan to brown to green with an off-white belly. The dewlap is orange with white spots.

This anole is found essentially throughout the island. In relatively open areas it is much more common than the bearded anole (*Anolis pogus*), while in forested areas it is less common. It has been suggested that it is less common at higher altitudes, but I believe this is simply because that is where most of the dense forest still exists. Even atop Pic Paradis, the highest point on the island, *Anolis gingivinus* is very common in open areas.

When fighting over territory, males change color dramatically, developing a dark patch behind the eye and accentuating their spots. They can also raise a large crest down their back that is not normally there. Other color variations seem to be related primarily to camouflage.

A tan coloration is not uncommon, and while the dorsal stripe may be subtle, the white stripes on the sides are almost always clearly visible.

A juvenile has adopted a greyish color to camouflage itself in rocky terrain.

This male has fully extended his dewlap to impress a nearby female, or perhaps to intimidate me. I was undeterred.

Males fight for choice territory on a stone wall. Note the extended dorsal ridges and exaggerated mottling that are common in aggressive displays.

Although primarily diurnal, this species can be seen hunting at night, particularly near artificial lights where insects congregate.

A testament to their ability to cling to branches, this individual was found dead, but still hanging from its final perch by a single forelimb.

A bearded anole (*Anolis pogus*) displaying grey coloration, pronounced banding and red eye coloration. Although they are often found on the ground, they may also be found on tree trunks and branches in the forest.

BEARDED ANOLE (*Anolis pogus*)

This anole is found only on St. Martin, although it once was also present on Anguilla and perhaps St. Barths. Until 1990, it was considered a subspecies of *Anolis wattsi*. Current species formerly grouped under *A. wattsi* include *A. wattsi*, which is native to Antigua and introduced to St. Lucia, Trinidad and Tobago, *A. forresti*, found on Barbuda and *A. schwartzi*, found on St. Eustatius, St. Kitts and Nevis. *A. schwartzi* and *A. forresti* are still considered subspecies of *A. wattsi* by some. The four species are very similar in appearance, and occupy analogous niches on their respective islands.

It is slightly smaller than the Anguilla bank anole, reaching a maximum SVL of about six centimeters. As it prefers shady areas, it most common on the forested hills and mountains, but can be found at sea level and even in developed areas if there is appropriate habitat. It is primarily seen on the ground or perched in the undergrowth or lower branches.

Coloration of this anole is highly variable. To some degree, the easiest way to identify it is by the lack of white bands on the sides. One common color pattern is tan with a turquoise patch around the eye. Darker brown and gray are also common, sometimes with light orange patches or bands. There may be a narrow, light dorsal stripe and irregular darker bands across the back, and these patterns vary from almost unnoticeable to very pronounced. The top of the head may be rust colored as well. In some cases the eye may be circled by red instead of turquoise, and when males are fighting for territory they may develop two black spots behind their eye. Like *Anolis gingivinus*, they are also capable of raising a crest down their back that is not normally present.

Anolis pogus exhibiting tan coloration and turquoise surrounding the eye. Dorsal stripe and banding across back are light, but clearly visible.

This coloration is more typical of dense forests where darker shades improve camouflage on bark and amongst leaf litter.

A specimen with a mottled red head and some banding, but no light-colored dorsal stripe. Changes in coloration are used for camouflage and communication, although the meanings are not well-understood.

This male has extended a dorsal ridge and partially expanded its dewlap as part of a display. The tip of the tail is also almost black, which is a often part of this display.

Males fighting over territory assume aggressive coloration, including double dark spots behind the eye. This battle lasted over ten minutes, starting at a perch six feet high and ending on the forest floor.

The same pair, still fighting a few minutes later, having changed to a strikingly different color and pattern.

Very dark coloration is relatively common in adult iguanas, which often appear near black. After this photo was taken, this individual dove into the water and I did not see it surface.

COMMON IGUANA (*Iguana iguana*)

The common, or green iguana is currently very common on St. Martin, but this was not always the case. Habitat destruction, mongoose predation and human consumption contributed to the extinction or near-extinction of this species on the island by the early 1990s. Since then, particularly in the last few years, they have either rebounded or re-colonized the island.

One account of the repopulation of Saint Martin involves a number of crates of live iguanas abandoned at the airport which were freed by sympathetic workers. During subsequent airport expansion, these iguanas were distributed to other mangrove wetlands around the island. Also, after hurricanes in 1995, a group of 15 iguanas adrift on a tangle of trees made an improbable overseas journey over 200 miles from Guadeloupe to Anguilla, where they were previously not found, suggesting the possibility of natural inter-island colonization.

The green iguana is easily distinguished from its smaller cousin, *Iguana delicatissima*, by the presence of a large subtympanic scale. This is a round scale found below the lower jaw and is present on both juveniles and adults. While young specimens are bright green, this coloration gives way to primarily brown coloration as the iguanas mature. Some specimens may also be reddish-orange or nearly black. Banding down the back and black rings around the tail are also typical of the species.

This species is most common in wetland areas, often roosting in mangroves at the edge of salt ponds. When approached, they frequently run directly into the water. I have seen them descend and either not surface for several minutes, or swim underwater to surface unseen in a mangrove thicket. I have also seen them swim across salt ponds at the surface. In the late afternoon, they may often be seen sunning themselves on rocks or even seaside cliff faces.

This individual was recently attacked by a dog while scavenging leftover vegetables behind a restaurant. Rather than running, it thrashed its tail as a defense mechanism when approached.

Lighter coloration in adults, including green, gray and orange hues is also common. Iguanas may often be seen perched on mangrove branches around salt ponds.

Juvenile iguanas are bright green, although this color fades as they age. Even at this early age, the subtympanic scale is visible, directly below the ear.

On the cliffs near Le Trou de David, groups of iguanas gather to bask in the late afternoon sunlight. They are quite adept at climbing, even on near-vertical cliff faces.

This very young juvenile iguana spent several minutes licking water droplets off leaves of grass after an afternoon rain shower.

A typical specimen of *Amieva plei analifera* rests on a rock a few feet from the beach. Most commonly seen in sunny roadside areas, individuals can also be seen hunting for insects on the beach.

ANGUILLA BANK AMIEVA (*Amieva plei analifera*)

Teiids from the genus *Amieva* are found on most of the islands in the Lesser Antilles. The species found on Saint Martin, *Amieva plei*, is also found on Anguilla and St. Barths, although the subspecies *analifera* is endemic to Saint Martin.

These ground-dwelling lizards are often quite large and, while fast, have an ungainly gait, skittering from side to side. Juveniles are typically brown with light stripes on the back running from behind the head to the hind legs. Both adults and juveniles typically have light spots from their hips down their tails. Some individuals have a greenish tint in the lower part of their body. Very large adults sometimes have black patches or bars on their shoulders, a characteristic that is only found in the Saint Martin subspecies.

These sun-loving lizards are often found on roadsides where they forage for insects and other invertebrates in the leaf litter. In some areas they may also be found at the edge of the beach. While they are often present in partially-forested areas, it is unusual to see them in dense forest.

While these lizards seem very common, because they are highly visible near human habitation, it is believed that their numbers are significantly suppressed by mongoose predation. On mongoose-free islands, *Amieva* are widespread, while on islands with mongoose populations, they tend to be restricted to developed areas that are avoided by mongoose. To some degree, it is possible that the continued development of Saint Martin offer some benefits to this lizard, but mongoose eradication would clearly be the preferred method for ensuring its survival.

This juvenile is typical of the St. Martin subspecies, where even young juveniles have faded or otherwise indistinct stripes down their back.

Some juveniles on St. Martin do have seven distinct stripes as this species does on other islands. It is unclear if this represents distinct populations, or a variable trait in the subspecies.

At night, the amieva hides in burrows under rocks and logs. As juveniles age, stripes on their back (if present) gradually fade until they disappear entirely.

Mid-sized adults typically have neither stripes nor black bars, but do have white or green speckling from the posterior down the tail.

The description of subspecies *analifera* typically references three to five black bars on the shoulders of large adults, which are only present in this subspecies. In the largest individuals more bars may be seen.

My research indicated that the satellite island Tintamarre is home to *A. plei plei*, the subspecies found on nearby islands, but not St. Martin. Specimens like this one do seem to have higher-contrast markings, but any differences seem subtle.

Sphaerodactylus parvus has a relatively narrow head and small eyes compared to other geckos, including the other local species of dwarf gecko, *Sphaerodactylus sputator*.

DWARF GECKO (*Sphaerodactylus parvus*)

This diminutive gecko was considered a subspecies of *Sphaerodactylus macrolepis* until 2001, when it was elevated to species status. It is found only on the islands of the Anguilla Bank: Anguilla, St. Martin and St. Barths. To my knowledge, there is no common name for this species.

Parvus is slightly smaller than *Sphaerodactylus sputator*, reaching a maximum SVL of about 3.5 cm. They are typically a medium brown with scattered dark spots on the back. Just behind the head, there is a distinctive dark oval with two light spots and usually a light ring around it. The head often has a pattern of dark bands. For a gecko, the head is quite narrow and the eyes are quite small.

This gecko is typically found in leaf litter in forested parts of the island. A very observant hiker may notice these occasionally, but they are easiest to find by lifting stones or pieces of log from the forest floor to uncover them (and replacing them gently afterwards). I have found that geckos seem to be more common beneath wood and lighter stones where there is decomposing leaf litter and abundant invertebrate life. Heavier stones sunk into the soil do not seem to be popular.

They can also be found around human habitation, typically beneath boards or stones in shady areas. Very small eggs, a half-centimeter or less in length, may also be found beneath stones in areas where these geckos live, although I don't know of any way to distinguish between the eggs of *sputator* and *parvus* without waiting for them to hatch.

Parvus coexists with *sputator*, and I have not discerned any difference in habits or preferred habitat. On the satellite islet Pinel, they are both quite common in the very limited amount of suitable habitat that exists.

Variation coloration and patterning in *parvus* is subtle. This individual is relatively light in color, but retains all the typical patterning of the species.

Leaf litter and other decaying organic matter is the preferred habitat for this species. Combined with its small size, this species can easily be overlooked, even where it is quite common.

While some descriptions of the species cite a yellowish head, this does not seem to be present in the St. Martin population.

This individual is my closest example of the purported yellowish facial coloration. It is possible that the St. Martin population is somewhat distinct from those on Anguilla and St. Barths.

Eggs are typically laid in protected concavities on the underside of rocks or logs. This particular egg may be that of *parvus* or *sputator*.

This specimen was found on the underside of a chunk of coral skeleton in a small, forested area of Pinel, a habitat that it shares with *S. parvus*. The orange hue of the tail, which is described only for the St. Martin population is not visible on this individual.

LEAST ISLAND GECKO (*Sphaerodactylus sputator*)

Sphaerodactylus sputator can be found on a half dozen islands, including Sombrero, Anguilla, St. Martin, St. Barths, St. Eustatius, St. Kitts and Nevis.

Typical coloration is grey with broken white stripes and dark bands on the back. An orangish tail and bronze iris are cited as characteristics that are specific to the population on St. Martin. Close inspection may reveal occasional raised red scales scattered around the body. This species has a very typical gecko shape, with very large eyes and a broad head.

Darker individuals may be confused with *S. parvus*, but the size of the eyes and shape of the head can aid with identification. Females may reach nearly four cm in SVL, slightly larger than *S. parvus*, but the difference is not noticeable unless one was to measure them, which would be challenging.

In my observation, the habits and preferred habitats of the two species of dwarf gecko are indistinguishable. *S. sputator* more closely resembles other dwarf geckos in the Lesser Antilles, while *S. parvus* is closely related to *S. macrolepis* which is present in Puerto Rico and Central America. This may indicate that the two species arrived at different times or from different directions.

In this close-up, several raised, orange-red scales can be seen on the head and neck.

This female has an egg clearly visible on her left side. This species lays one egg at a time, and that egg is extremely large compared to the adult body size.

This individual is seen in the remains of a plastic cup, illustrating the typical size of an adult. The orange tail and bronze eye typical to the St. Martin population are visible in this individual.

Until I encountered this juvenile, I had assumed that the description of an orange tail meant an orangish cast. To date, this is the only one I have encountered with a truly orange tail. The white patterns are also distinctively yellow on this individual.

This particularly dark individual was found only a few meters from some of the much lighter specimens pictured on this page.

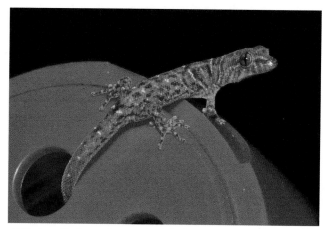

This juvenile is resting on the lid of a small spice jar. The hole where its tail is resting is approximately 6mm in diameter.

TROPICAL HOUSE GECKO (*Hemi-dactylus mabouya*)

This medium-sized gecko (up to 7 cm in SVL) is native to sub-Saharan Africa, but now lives in tropical areas of North, Central and South America as well as most islands in the Caribbean. It was likely introduced to the Americas inadvertently.

Coloration can vary dramatically, from very pale or pinkish with few visible markings to a mottled grey or brown coloration. It is often seen at night in or around homes and other buildings, but can also be found under boards or rocks in some grassy areas. Eggs are typically laid in pairs in rotting wood or beneath stones.

Like other geckos, minute setae (hair-like bristles) on their toe pads give them the ability to easily climb vertical surfaces. This gecko also has the ability to spontaneously drop its tail when frightened to distract predators.

While these insectivores are welcome guests in many homes, it is unknown what negative impact they may have on native species.

Locally geckos are often called woodslaves. Their climbing abilities have inspired a local legend that if you get one on your skin you need to use a hot iron to remove it because it will stick too strongly to remove it otherwise.

This individual is surprised to find his home (a discarded wooden gate) suddenly lifted. This mottled gray coloration is typical of individuals living in grassland areas.

This very pale individual is seen perched near the roof of a home. Despite their speed and agility, they are very wary of humans and quickly flee when approached.

An individual with a necrotic tail. Presumably it had attempted to drop its tail but it had not completely detached.

This newly-hatched juvenile is approximately two centimeters long. Shortly before hatching, one can feel the movement of the baby inside the egg.

UNDERWOOD'S SPECTACLED TEGU
(*Gymnophthalmus underwoodi*)

This lizard is a microteiid, and is similar in size to the dwarf geckos. Its previously described range includes parts of Central and South America as well as a number of islands in the Lesser Antilles, although none particularly near St. Martin. I would guess that it is a relatively recent introduction to St. Martin, done inadvertently by man.

These lizards have a shiny tan back with darker sides and an elongated body shape with a very long tail. It could be possible to confuse them with a young skink (if there are any on the island) or ground lizard, but I think it is unlikely. If in doubt, identification may be confirmed by the presence of only four toes on the front feet.

Typical habitats for these lizards are sunny grassland areas or scrublands. They may be seen beneath rotting logs in open areas, but they also forage openly in the grass. Due to their small size they may easily be overlooked.

This curious lizard is unisexual and reproduces parthenogenically. This may be a key factor in its ability to colonize new islands, as a single individual can reproduce to start a new population.

This lizard is named after Garth Underwood, a pioneering British herpetologist responsible for much important work on reptiles in the Caribbean, including significant revisions to the taxonomy of *Anolis* species of the Lesser Antilles in the late 1950s.

A related species, *Gymnophthalmus pleei*, is found on some of the Lesser Antilles and is quite similar in appearance, but is not known to reside on St. Martin. It has ridged scales on the tail, which offer a subtle point of differentiation. As its range includes other French West Indies (Martinique and Guadeloupe), it would not be too surprising for *G. pleei* to arrive in the future as an accidental introduction.

This individual was found in a grassy roadside area near Étang Guichard. The lack of ridged scales on the tail helps distinguish it from *G. pleei*.

Microteiids have transparent lower eyelids, allowing them to see with their eyes closed. This characteristic is what led them to be called spectacled lizards.

In this photo, the presence of only four toes on the front feet is clearly noticeable, as is the extremely long tail.

BRAHMINY BLIND SNAKE (*Ramphotyphlops braminus*)

This strange-looking snake is native to Africa and Asia, but has been introduced to many areas around the world. Sometimes called the flowerpot snake, it is thought that this species has been introduced in part through stowaways traveling in potted tropical plants. It is probably introduced to Saint Martin only recently.

This snake is very small, reaching only about 17 cm in length, and has a worm-like appearance. It is, however, a surprisingly fast mover. Its eyes are rudimentary and are covered with scales, limiting its vision. They seem to sense light and darkness, but probably nothing more than that. The tail is quite short and may be hard to distinguish from the head.

This species may have a limited range, and I have primarily seen them in Grand Case. They are typically found under stones, bricks or boards, but apparently may be seen in the open after heavy rain. When captured, they thrash violently and excrete a smelly substance from a pair of glands near the base of the tail to discourage predators.

Like *Gymnophthalmus underwoodi*, this species is parthenogenic, and all specimens collected have been female. Several other species of blind snake are present in the Caribbean, but none are recorded on Saint Martin.

An adult specimen seen with a quarter for scale. Juvenile specimens I have seen are several times smaller.

In this closer view of the head the rudimentary eye can be seen as a dark spot beneath translucent scales.

Although it is usually hiding during the day, the blind snake may occasionally be seen hunting at night. This one was crawling across a stone wall in search of invertebrate prey.

The tail is very short and comes to a sharp point at the end. When fleeing predators, this snake tends to move both ends similarly, perhaps to cause confusion about which end is which.

RED-FOOTED TORTOISE (*Geochelone carbonaria*)

This is the only species of tortoise found in the Lesser Antilles. Native to South America, it may have been introduced by Arawak or Caribe settlers as a food source before European colonization, or perhaps later either for food or as escaped pets. This genus also includes the giant tortoises of the Galapagos islands.

This medium-sized tortoise is typically 25 to 35 cm in carapace-length and can easily be identified by the yellow and orange spots in the center of the plates on the back of its shell, as well as the yellow to red scales on its face and limbs. The shell is somewhat rectangular, but mature specimens tend to develop a noticeable "waist" mid-shell which gives them an hourglass appearance.

Their round, brittle eggs, which are laid in small clutches, may be eaten by mongoose and rats. Their natural habitat is ranges from forest to grassland areas, and their diet is omnivorous, including carrion as well as fruits and plants.

This species does not seem to be particularly common. I have seen one individual crossing a path in a scrubby area of Pinel and know that they are present on Goat Mountain. In the past, they were common on Tintamarre as well, but are now thought to be rare there, the majority being taken home for pets, or dinner. There are apparently a great many of these turtles in captivity on the island, and they breed readily in this situation.

This individual was probably a young adult, approximately 25 cm in carapace length. Its ability to last long periods without food or water is probably an advantage during the dry season on St. Martin.

This specimen was seen in the late morning. Typically, they are active in the morning and evening, seeking shelter during the midday heat.

There are many varieties of this tortoise throughout its range, although none have been formally classified as distinct species as yet.

This specimen of the Cuban treefrog was apprehended at the Marigot gendarmerie, where it was hunting inside the office. A single dropping made while under our supervision indicated that it had recently eaten a large cockroach.

AMPHIBIANS

Having permeable skin is a significant barrier to oceanic colonization. The relative lack of permanent freshwater bodies on St. Martin also makes it a difficult place for amphibians. Not surprisingly, there are only a few species of amphibian on St. Martin.

There are three species of frog on the island which I have seen. The coqui antillano (*Eleutherodactylus johnstonei*) is a whistling frog, and it is possible that a similar species, *E. martinicensis* has also been recently introduced. The two-striped treefrog (*Scinax rubra*) is a slightly larger treefrog that was probably introduced but has been on the island for decades. The Cuban treefrog (*Osteopilus septentrionalis*) is much larger and seems to have been introduced quite recently. In general, all the frogs are more easily heard than seen.

This two-striped treefrog grew up with hundreds of others in an unused swimming pool in Cul de Sac. Its facial deformities may be the result of pollution, or perhaps just the pressure of trying to mature quickly with hundreds of cannibalistic siblings.

COQUI ANTILLANO (*Eleutherodactylus johnstonei*)

Several species from this family are naturally occurring in the Lesser Antilles, with one species living on St. Martin. This small frog is heard more often than seen, but does seem to be locally common in hospitable areas. Although not a true treefrog, it is typically arboreal. The maximum adult size is less than four cm SVL. This species lays clusters of relatively large eggs covered in mucus which hatch directly into small froglets, bypassing the tadpole stage. This frog is also known as Johnstone's whistling frog.

This juvenile blends into his environment remarkably well. He was seen on Pic Paradis, hopping around the leaf litter on the forest floor.

In this photo of an adult coqui, the v-shaped mark above the shoulders is clearly visible. (Photo taken in Saba.)

Immature coqui may be very small, since they emerge from their eggs as tiny froglets. This individual was only a few millimeters long. (Photo taken in Saba.)

Compared to the other frogs on the island, the coqui is generally darker and has more distinct markings, although all species seem to be somewhat variable and capable of changing color depending on their mood.

TWO-STRIPED TREEFROG (*Scinax rubra*)

This species of South American treefrog is thought to be introduced by man, and only one species from this family is present in the Lesser Antilles. It is larger than the coqui antillano.

Tadpoles of this species are easily found in most puddles and other freshwater bodies, although they seem relatively rare in the roadside ditches that are home to guppies. In developed areas, anthropogenic rainwater caches (such as abandoned swimming pools) serve as breeding locations.

The tadpoles of this species are brown but may look black, particularly in poor lighting or dirty water. As they mature, they become cannibalistic. Tiny hind legs are visible.

This two-striped tree frog has recently transformed from a tadpole. A full-sized adult can be several times larger.

This individual is transitioning into a frog. While their hind legs are visible for some time, once their front legs come out (after developing under the skin), the transformation to a frog takes only a couple days.

The most distinctive feature of this species are the light lines running down each side of the body. The back varies from dark brown to shiny gold.

This young frog is absorbing the last of his tail, but his facial structure and coloration are not yet fully developed.

CUBAN TREEFROG (*Osteopilus septentrionalis*)

The Cuban treefrog is a relatively recent introduction to the island, and is several times larger than the other frogs, six to twelve centimeters in length. A notorious stowaway, it has been introduced accidentally to many islands in the Caribbean.

They are known to be voracious eaters, and it is probable that the other frogs on the island make up a good part of their diet, along with insects and other small animals.

Males have dark, callus-like patches on their thumbs which help them grip the female during sex.

The Cuban tree frog has very large toe pads, and the skin over its skull is fused to the skull to reduce moisture loss.

During the day, I found many Cuban treefrogs sleeping in the small pools of water held by bromeliads. When inactive, they were often almost white.

This frog often has two dark stripes down its back, but these are not always visible, or may be broken into a series of splotches. The areas in the folds of the legs are often bright yellow.

After his photo shoot, this Cuban treefrog was released. Although they are an invasive species, the fate of a single individual is probably insignificant to their ability to remain established on the island.

This large katydid (*Nesonotus* sp.), with its striking and alien appearance, is just one example of the fascinating and peculiar diversity of insect life on the island. This specimen was found hiding in the hollow of a tree in the forest near the top of Pic Paradis.

INSECTS

The class Insecta is incredibly diverse, including more than a million known species, which probably only represents a small fraction of the total species. In fact, the number of described insect species outnumbers that of all other animals combined.

Past research has documented over 100 species of insect on the island, although the true number of species is surely at least several times greater. As most insects are able to fly, they have colonized St. Martin quite successfully.

Insects have colonized every imaginable habitat on St. Martin, from the seaside to the mountaintops. While some are ubiquitous, others may only be encountered in their preferred habitats. The temperature of the island is relatively consistent, allowing for year-round activity, but many species are noticeably more common during the rainier months when vegetation is more lush.

In this section, butterflies and moths (Lepidoptera) are covered in detail. This is possible because their attractiveness has made them perhaps the most studied group of insects. Less popular orders are included in less detail, largely due to a relative lack of available research.

The enormous diversity of insects compared to other animals often makes specific identification difficult or even impossible, but hopefully the photographs included in this section will give the reader some idea of the myriad of fascinating and often beautiful species present on St. Martin.

LEPIDOPTERA

This insect order contains over 180,000 species of butterflies and moths, of which close to 30 species of butterfly and likely over 100 species of moth are present on the island. These insects have a complicated life cycle, from egg to caterpillar to pupa to adult. Caterpillars typically have specific host plants from which many derive toxins to make them distasteful to predators. The lack of mountains high enough to sustain a cloud forest limits the diversity of this order on St. Martin compared to newer, more mountainous islands in the Lesser Antilles.

Butterfly chrysalides are typically bare, like these of the cloudless sulfur, while many moths encase their pupae in silken cocoons. If touched gently, they may wiggle.

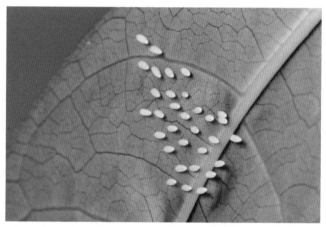

Butterfly and moth eggs are small and inconspicuous. They are typically laid on the leaves of the preferred host plant. Different species may have one, several or many host plants.

Many butterflies and moths are subject to parasitism, often by ichneumon wasps and tachinid flies, which deposit eggs inside living caterpillars. The larvae feed on the living host animal. This monarch chrysalis was probably parasitized by tachinid flies.

Caterpillars vary widely in appearance, from relatively camouflaged, like this cloudless sulfur, to brightly-colored, warning of inedibility. Some species also change appearance as they grow and molt.

This section is dedicated to our beloved Crêpe, who was maimed during his pupation by a very unpleasant young child who threw his chrysalis on the ground. We miss you!

The tropical checkered skipper (*Pyrgus oileus*), is a diminutive delight found primarily in grassy fields. Along with several other species on the island, it is a spread-winged skipper (subfamily Pyrginae), a group named for their habit of basking with wings spread open.

BUTTERFLIES

The abundance of butterflies contributes greatly to the charm and beauty of the island. The few larger species are most obvious, but the many smaller species may in fact be more rewarding to the dedicated lepidopterist.

Close to thirty species of butterfly have been documented on the island, most of which are included here. Most species breed year-round, although many are less common during the relatively dry period of late winter and early spring. While most seem to prefer sunny, open areas, a few species, particularly amongst the skippers, are more common in the forest.

It is likely that the island has lost a few species of butterfly as a result of habitat destruction and spraying to control mosquitoes. Several species that are still present on nearby islands were probably once found on St. Martin. St. Martin has also been colonized by at least one invasive species, the checkered swallowtail. Occasional vagrants from species with no local breeding population may be observed from occasionally as well.

An unidentified skipper, possibly *Euphyes* sp., sips nectar from a morning glory flower. It is one of several butterfly species I have seen only once or twice on the island.

MONARCH (*Danaus plexippus*)

Multiple subspecies of monarch may be present on the island, the migratory North American (*D. p. plexippus*) and a non-migratory subspecies found from Florida to the Amazon river (*D. p. megalippe*). It is also likely that the two subspecies interbreed, making them difficult to distinguish. Caterpillars and chrysalides are most commonly found on the apple of Sodom (*Calotropis procera*), a dogbane related to milkweed that grows into bushes up to six meters in height. I have also observed them feeding on the Mexican butterfly weed (*Asclepias curassavica*), a smaller plant from the same family. The photographs on this page depict each stage of this butterfly's life cycle.

Monarch caterpillars have distinctive yellow, white and black stripes as well as a pair of fleshy tentacles at each end. The poisonous milky sap of the plant makes it distasteful to predators.

Monarchs begin mating in mid-air, but the process typically takes several hours, most of which they spend perched on trees or plants.

Monarch chrysalides are found on the underside of the leaves of their host plant. Brown chrysalids with small holes in them are found when parasitic wasps have eaten the pupa and emerged.

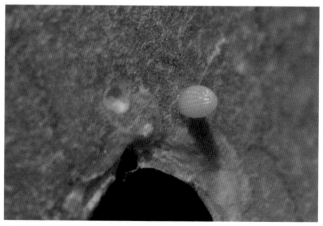

A female monarch repeatedly alighting upon apple of Sodom leaves may be laying eggs, which are deposited singly.

A newly-emerged adult monarch perches on its host plant while its wings harden. This moment is perhaps the best time to get a close-up photograph.

VISITORS AND FUGITIVES

There are several species of butterfly that I have seen only once on the island. The black swallowtail (*Papilio polyxenes*) is not documented as a resident of the Lesser Antilles, but is known to be a strong flyer with a range extending to the Bahamas. However, I have been told that it is very unlikely that it would be able to get here on its own. The mimic (*Hypolimnas misippus*) comes from Africa, Asia and Australia, but does breed on some islands in the Caribbean. It is possible that it was introduced during the slave trade, or established itself from individuals blown across the ocean from Africa. The individual I encountered does not necessarily indicate they breed on St. Martin.

The Indian leafwing (*Kallima paralekta*) that I found on St. Martin was surely an escapee from The Butterfly Farm, a small tourist attraction that raises a variety of non-native butterfly species. Considering the farm has been open for fifteen years, I would guess that if any escaped species had become established in the wild they would be more noticeable. Although this is likely a single escapee, it is included here on the chance that it does find a larval food source and begin breeding on the island.

The painted lady (*Vanessa cardui*) is known to be a great wanderer and has been found on many Caribbean islands, although it is not known to be a breeding resident.

The black swallowtail is found throughout most of North America and northern South America. This individual was seen at the top of Pic Paradis.

This male mimic was seen near Bell Point on a forested hilltop. It may be a visitor from a neighboring island.

The painted lady is found on all continents except Antarctica and South America, making it an unsurprising visitor to St. Martin and other Caribbean islands.

This Indian leafwing was seen in a densely forested area not far from The Butterfly Farm.

CHECKERED SWALLOWTAIL (*Papilio demoleus*)

Also known as the lime or citrus swallowtail, this Asian species was first documented in the Caribbean in 2004 on Hispaniola. On Saint Martin, it is seasonally quite common, at least in some areas. It is considered a serious pest to citrus farmers, and its impact on the native plants and animals of the island is as yet unknown. I have personally observed the caterpillars eating every single bit of leaf and stem from a tree stump that had sprouted a number of new branches. Eventually, the larger caterpillars pupated, and many of the smaller ones left the stump in search of other edible vegetation. Even then, adults circled the barren stump, interested in depositing more eggs.

Early instar caterpillars of this species have coloration that resembles bird droppings as a form of protective camouflage. If disturbed they may extrude a pair of tentacles from each end.

Later instar caterpillars of the checkered swallowtail are green with dark stripes and colorful spots. If threatened, they rear up and extrude two orange-red tentacles.

The adult checkered swallowtail is quite beautiful. This recently hatched specimen was just learning to fly, fluttering uneasily and falling to the ground multiple times.

Preparing to pupate, this caterpillar has created a sling of silk to hold itself upright. In the background a small branch has been picked clean.

TROPICAL BUCKEYE (*Junonia genoveva*) AND MANGROVE BUCKEYE (*Junonio evarete*)

These two very similar species of buckeye are found throughout the Caribbean and are relatively common on St. Martin. It is quite difficult or even impossible to distinguish the two species by casual observation. The tropical buckeye has darker, more pronounced spots on the underside of the hindwing and a broad white patch above the large spot on the upper of the forewing. Aside from these small differences, the pattern and coloration of the two species are basically the same. In fact, historically the two species have often been confused and the common name mangrove buckeye has been used for both species.

The mangrove buckeye is, not surprisingly, common in wetland areas near mangroves, and its caterpillars are known to feed on black mangrove (*Avicennia germinans*). The tropical buckeye may be seen in any sunny area, and its caterpillars are known to feed on various types of Verbena and Acanthus plants.

These mangrove buckeyes were seen on a mud flat in wetlands near mangroves. The large white patch on the forewing is clearly absent.

This tropical buckeye has the distinctive white patch just above the large spot on the forewing.

This tropical buckeye is feeding from Mexican creeper (*Antigonon leptopus*) flowers.

The tropical buckeye caterpillar is black with six rows of hairy bristles which are blue on the back and orange on the sides. Very small yellow or white dots and lines are present as well.

The first specimen encountered was heavily damaged, which could be an indication that it had traveled from another island.

The gulf fritillary frequents sunny areas where it feeds on the nectar of various flowers. It is difficult to approach and quick to flit away, although they often circle back.

The pattern and general shape of the wings resembles the local buckeye species, although the white peacock has small lobes extending from the hindwings.

The underside of the gulf fritillary is orange-brown with a pattern of white or silvery blotches.

WHITE PEACOCK (*Anartia jatrophae*)

The white peacock is similar in pattern to the buckeye species, but markedly different in coloration. To date, I have only seen a handful on the island, which may indicate that the species is quite rare, or that the individuals I observed were vagrants from another island. Multiple sightings were near a salt pond and mangrove area, which is likely their preferred habitat.

There are several subspecies, including a half-dozen in the Caribbean. *A. j. jatrophae* is the subspecies found in the Lesser Antilles.

GULF FRITILLARY (*Agraulis vanillae*)

This is the only species of heliconian I have seen on St. Martin. With a variety of other species on neighboring islands, it is likely that St. Martin was formerly home to additional species from this subfamily. Perhaps small populations of other species exist here even today.

The gulf fritillary is quite common and easily identified by its medium size and bright orange coloration. The caterpillars are known to feed on passion flower (*Passiflora* spp.), thus becoming poisonous to predators. The caterpillar is bright orange with several rows of long, black bristles, essentially matching the color scheme of the adult.

GREAT SOUTHERN WHITE (*Ascia monuste virginia*)

This butterfly is the most visible and probably the most common butterfly on the island. The subspecies *virginia* is found throughout the northern Lesser Antilles. Predominantly white with black markings on the tips of the forewings, the underside of the rear wing and tip of the forewing are yellow in males. The underside of the wings on the female may be mostly white, light yellow, or white with gray patterns. The caterpillar is dark with yellow stripes, black spots and numerous small hairs that are black on top and white on the sides. Not a fussy eater, groups of eggs are laid on a variety of host plants.

This feeding female exhibits the darker coloration variant. It is suggested that this is tied to the wet season, but this is does not seem consistent on St. Martin.

In this mating couple the male is below and the lighter-colored female is above.

Large groups are often found drinking water from mud or cow dung. If approached, they erupt into a fluttering cloud but quickly regroup and resume drinking.

Clusters of elongated yellow eggs are found on a variety of host plants.

This male is almost completely white, although the thin dark line around the front of the forewing is visible. The angularity of the wings helps to distinguish this species from *A. monuste*.

The female cloudless sulfur is not entirely cloudless. In addition to the distinctive pair of spots on the hindwing, a bit of the dark edge of the forewing can be seen in this photo.

Distinguishing females from *A. monuste* is even more difficult, but the shape of the wings is still subtly distinctive. The hindwing has a more angular border and the bottom extends to a slight point.

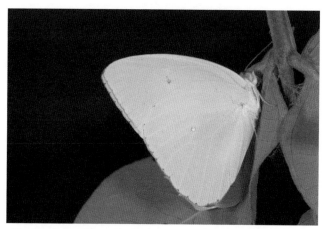

The male cloudless sulfur is almost entirely yellow. This specimen was recently hatched. In the field, this species is difficult to approach, but occasionally it will remain still while feeding.

FLORIDA WHITE (*Appias drusilla*)

Easily overlooked amongst the masses of great southern whites, the Florida white is paler and has more angular wings. The male has almost completely white wings with a fine line around the front of the forewing and some light shading on the underside of the wings. The forewings of the female have a small black border, while the underside is very light. In both sexes there is often some yellow at the base of the wings where they meet the body. There are a number of described subspecies, including several in the Caribbean. The population on St. Martin is most likely *boydi*.

CLOUDLESS SULFUR (*Phoebis sennae*)

The only large sulfur I have seen on the island, this species is a brilliant yellow and generally a bit larger than the great southern white. Males are almost totally devoid of markings, while females have a smattering of pink and a distinctive pair of white spots ringed with pink on the hind wings. The upper forewings of the female also have a dark border around the front. Chrysalides are light green and sharply angled, and the caterpillars are yellow and ribbed with a pairs of black ribs separated by four yellow ribs.

See page 53 for photos of the caterpillar and chrysalis of this species.

Hall's sulfur has distinctive markings on the tips of each wing. It is also noticeably larger than the other small sulfurs and is more likely to feed on the flowers of shrubs rather than undergrowth.

The identifying characteristics on the upper side of the wings are rarely visible when the false barred yellow is feeding (inset), but can be seen in flight or with a lucky gust of wind.

A mating pair of little yellows has chosen an inconspicuous spot amidst the grass. I believe the slightly darker butterfly on top is the male, but in this species have very similar coloration.

HALL'S SULFUR (*Eurema leuce*), FALSE BARRED YELLOW (*Eurema elathea*) AND LITTLE YELLOW (*Eurema lisa*)

At least three species from the genus *Eurema* are found on St. Martin. They are all quite small, four centimeters or less in wingspan and are relatively weak flyers that tend to stick close to the ground and are easily swept away in a brisk breeze.

Hall's sulfur is the largest and the female can be identified by patches of pink and brown at the edge of the underside of each wing. The underside of the male is almost all yellow, and both have a dark border on the front edge of the upper forewing.

The false barred yellow is primarily white. Both sexes have dark borders on the upper side of each wing and the male has yellow forewings with a pronounced black bar at the bottom.

The little yellow has a pink spot on the underside of the hindwing in both sexes, scattered dark spots and zigzags near the front edge of the hindwing. Each wing underside has a pink and white border with black spots at the end of each vein.

Other species that may also be present are the barred yellow (*Eurema daira*) which is very similar to *elathea*, and the little yellowie (*Eurema venusta*), which is similar to *leuce*.

The cassius blue has a range that extends from the southern United States to parts of South America. It is also called the tropical striped blue.

Once common in Florida, the Miami blue was thought to be extinct there in 1992. A group estimated at less than fifty individuals was found 1999. Additional colonies were found in 2006.

The hanno blue has a smaller range, primarily Central America, the Caribbean and a few northern parts of South America.

The males of all three species of blue tend to be primarily blue on the upperside of the wings. This specimen is a hanno blue, identified by photos showing the underside of the wings.

CASSIUS BLUE (*Leptotes cassius*), HANNO BLUE (*Hemiargus hanno*) AND MIAMI BLUE (*Cyclargus thomasi*)

Often only two centimeters in wingspan, these three blues, along with the similarly-sized hairstreaks, are the smallest butterflies on the island. They tend to fly low, rarely above waist height, and may frequently be seen feeding from small flowers. In the male, the upperside of each species is predominantly blue. Females have blue close to the body, but may also have light patches and a dark border around the wings.

The underside of the cassius blue is white with a gray-brown pattern of spots and bars with two pronounced eyespots at the rear of the hindwing. The subspecies here is probably *cassioides*, which is found in the Caribbean.

The underside of the hanno blue is predominantly gray, with one eyespot on the hindwing and two small black spots near the leading edge of the hindwing. The local subspecies is probably *watsoni*.

The Miami blue has two large eyespots and is essentially gray with white patches on its underside. There are several black spots on the hindwing, including two large ones near the leading edge. The local subspecies is likely to be *woodruffi*. The name Miami blue may also be used in reference to the critically endangered subspecies *bethunebakeri*, which is found only in Florida.

The angerona hairstreak can be identified by the thin black and white line running down its wings.

The columella scrub hairstreak has generous splashes of orange and red near its tail.

This disjunct scrub hairstreak appears to be laying eggs.

Hairstreak caterpillars are often oval-shaped, with the head only visible from the underside. They are known to feed on various plants in the mallow family, including hibiscus.

ANGERONA HAIRSTREAK (*Electrostrymon angerona*), DISJUNCT SCRUB HAIRSTREAK (*Strymon bubastus ponce*) AND COLUMELLA SCRUB HAIRSTREAK (*Strymon columella*)

St. Martin is home to at least three species of hairstreak. Belonging to family Lycaenidae with the blues on the previous page, they are similar in size and habit and quite difficult to identify in flight.

The angerona hairstreak has tan wing undersides with a thin white and black stripe going down both wings and long tails.

The disjunct scrub hairstreak has no tails and is actually quite similar to the hanno blue, but more tan in color and with a pronounced orange shading on many of the spots.

The columella scrub hairstreak has two patches of orange and red on the hindwings near the its tails. It is sometimes called Hewitson's hairstreak.

SKIPPERS (HESPERIIDAE)

There are several thousand species of skipper, including at least six on St. Martin. Identification can be quite difficult. In fact, many species can only be distinguished through dissection and microscopic evaluation of the genitalia. I have not done this. I do believe, however, that the identifications made here are likely to be correct, or at least pretty close. I believe there are also at least two resident species I have not yet identified.

With their thick bodies, hooked antennae and large eyes, these butterflies often resemble moths and are, in fact, typically classified in a separate superfamily from the rest of the butterflies.

This individual has assumed a typical pose while feeding from small flowers in a sunlit clearing in the forest.

The sugar cane skipper (*Panoquina sylvicola*) is found on many Caribbean islands. This female was laying eggs on blades of grass, although this species also uses sugar cane as a host plant.

The underside of the tropical checkered skipper is similar to the upper surface, although the rear wing is white with irregular, gray bars with black outlines.

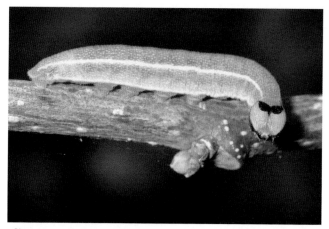

Skipper caterpillars typically have a large, round head, often black or yellow.

TROPICAL CHECKERED SKIPPER (*Pyrgus oileus*)

This small skipper, less than four centimeters in wingspan, is quite common on the island and can be seen feeding in sunny areas. Gray-brown with white markings that form irregular bands, they are often perched with wings spread, either to capture sunlight for energy or, if male, to attract females. The species ranges from the southern United States to Argentina. Like many skippers, the body and inner portion of the wings are furry, with gray-blue hairs on this species.

Iridescent blue-green coloration in the furry area of the body and inner wings distinguishes this species from other long-tailed skippers.

The hammock skipper has less intense, but still noticeable, blue-green on the body and a set of three large and three small white spots on the forewing.

The long tails help to distinguish this skipper from the hammock skipper, which has similar coloration and patterning.

The single black spot and purple sheen on the underside of the wings help distinguish the hammock skipper from a number of other similar species.

LONG-TAILED SKIPPER (*Urbanus proteus*)

This skipper has a wingspan of up to six centimeters, and is the largest skipper on the island. It is easily identified by the brilliant blue-green coloration on the body and inner wings and its long tails. Although there are several other tailed species in the Caribbean, they do not have the iridescent blue-green.

This skipper seems to prefer border zones between forested and open areas and is often found feeding in meadows and perching on nearby trees.

HAMMOCK SKIPPER (*Polygonus leo*)

This skipper is similar in habit to the long-tailed skipper. It does not have tails, but does have noticeable lobes on the rear wings. The underside of the rear wing has a single black spot, and both wings tend to have a purplish sheen.

This fast-flyer often rests on the underside of leaves and also seems most common on the edge between forested and open areas, or near clearings and trails.

The male is essentially solid black, but flashes iridescent purple when sunlight hits at the right angle.

The key distinguishing mark on this skipper is the vaguely v-shaped mark on the forewing.

The female is similar to the hammock skipper, but has a different pattern of white spots on its forewing tips. It also lacks the lobes that are present on the rear wings of the hammock skipper.

With its wings folded together, this skipper is difficult to identify. The thin black line near the edge of the wing is the only significant characteristic.

CARIBBEAN DUSKYWING (*Ephyriades arcas*)

These skippers seem to prefer forested areas, and can be seen on narrow trails as well. The upperside of the male is black with a purple or dark blue sheen, while the underside is typically brown. Generally there are no markings on either side. Females are brown and somewhat similar to the hammock skipper, but darker and with no green patch. They have similar white spots near the forewing tips, but near the three large spots, there is a fourth smaller one and instead of a line of three small spots, there are six.

VITELLIUS SKIPPER (*Choranthus vitellius*)

There are a number of similar species in this genus, of which *vitellius* is the best match both in appearance and in geography. With a number of species and subspecies defined that are endemic to specific islands, including two new species discovered on Hispaniola in 1983, it is likely that the taxonomy of these skippers is subject to change.

These skippers are found primarily in sunny areas, but I have also seen them resting near lights at night. They are part of a subfamily known as grass skippers which contains over 2,000 species.

Sphacelodes vulneraria, known as the looper moth, is a medium-sized Geometrid. A general lack of research concerning the moths of the Caribbean makes identification difficult at times, but also represents an opportunity for discovery.

MOTHS

I would guess there are well over 100 species of moth on the island. There are thousands of species in the Caribbean and I have seen more than 50 without even attempting to do a comprehensive investigation. Scientific research on the topic is far from complete.

There are a handful of diurnal moths that may be seen while exploring the island, but the majority are nocturnal. Although they may easily be overlooked, the moths of the island are tremendously varied and often quite interesting.

In this section there are detailed accounts of a few of the more noticeable species followed by photographs of some representative types, identified as closely as possible.

LEAVE THE LIGHT ON

One of the most effective ways to study moths and other nocturnal insects is to leave an outdoor light on at night. In this manner I have been able to study a wide variety of species quite conveniently. The ideal set-up is a bright light on white walls that reflect the light and also make it easier to see specimens. A white sheet may also be used. For the truly ambitious, ultraviolet lights are particularly effective at attracting moths.

For reasons unknown to me, the light on our sea-facing back veranda invariably attracts larger numbers and more diversity of species than that on our land-facing front veranda. Both lights are of comparable wattage, and neither is obstructed in any way.

TETRIO SPHINX (*Pseudosphinx tetrio*) AND OTHER SPHINGIDAE

This large sphingid is perhaps most noticeable during the larval stage. Huge, brightly-colored caterpillars may be seen completely stripping frangipani bushes of their leaves (typically just before the plants shed them to conserve water during the dry season). The large pupae are typically found in the dirt below host plants.

The adult sphinx moths are stout, fast-flying moths and are often quite large. A number of species are present on the island. Unlike most moths, many species are diurnal nectar-feeders. In flight or while hovering to feed from flowers they may be mistaken for hummingbirds.

This newly-hatched sphinx is probably *Pachylia ficus*, one of the larger species on the island.

Tetrio sphinx caterpillars feed on frangipani, which grows both wild and in gardens. They reach over fifteen cm in length and often completely denude their host plant.

This specimen (probably *P. tetrio*) was partially eaten and had no abdomen. Perhaps due to their large size, they are more than a meal for the typical island insectivore.

Several species of sphinx, like this *Erinnyis ello*, have brightly-colored hindwings.

The adult is not particularly moth-like in flight and casual observers often mistake it for a beetle or bee.

Caterpillars are quite common, and noticeable, on oleander bushes. Despite their abundance, only in extreme cases do they defoliate the entire host plant.

Although it is difficult to see in this photo, the eyespot on the inner forewing is in the shape of a 9 or a large comma (backwards on the right wing).

BLACK WITCH (*Ascalapha odorata*)

This moth is a harbinger of death in some Caribbean folklore, and is also the largest moth on the island by wing size at up to sixteen cm in wingspan. This nocturnal moth spends its days hiding on rocks or trees in shady areas. It is particularly common in the dry gullies that run down the forested mountains, and will take flight briefly when passed closely. Due to its size and coloration it is easy to briefly mistake it for a bat, and in fact, it is often called a bat by locals. With their excellent camouflage and reclusive habits, they are difficult to find, approach and photograph.

SPOTTED OLEANDER CATERPILLAR MOTH (*Empyreuma affinis*)

Although this moth is native to the Caribbean, it is a relatively recent introduction to St. Martin, first noticed locally in the 1980s, around the same time as introductions were documented on other Caribbean islands and in Florida. The widespread planting of its larval host plant, oleander (*Nerium oleander*), in gardens and on roadsides undoubtedly contributes to its success on the island.

This stocky moth is often seen flying clumsily during the day and the bright orange caterpillars are easy to find on oleander bushes.

Ornate moths are common in grassy areas. Startled adults briefly take flight, but once they find a suitable perch it is often possible to approach them quite closely.

The hieroglyphic moth is brightly colored, with intricate patterns of orange, yellow, blue and black.

Larvae feed on rattlepod (*Crotalaria* spp.), preferring the unripe seeds, which they eat from within the seed pods. Toxic alkaloids concentrated in the seeds make the caterpillars inedible.

Caterpillars are quite large, and many of them may be seen feeding near each other on the same host plant.

ORNATE MOTH (*Utetheisa ornatrix*)

Also called the bella moth, this species may be seen in grassy areas during the day, making short flights when disturbed. In flight, it appears white, but it has a black and red design around the forewing, and a black border surrounding white or pink on the hindwing.

Highly variable in appearance, variations were considered to be two species until a recent consolidation under *ornatrix*. On the island, the inner portion of the forewing may be almost entirely white, or may have red markings and black spots.

HIEROGLYPHIC MOTH (*Diphthera festiva*)

This moth may be seen at rest during the day on leaves, trees or walls. While not uncommon, they are not particularly visible, considering their caterpillars feed on a variety of plants that are quite plentiful on the island.

The caterpillar of this species is white with an irregular grid of black lines. The head, rear and prolegs (the fleshy leg-like structures on the abdomen) are bright red. They feed on a variety of shrubs in the mallow family (Malvaceae).

ADDITIONAL MOTHS

The following pages contain a sampling of the many varied moths that are found on St. Martin. Identification and additional information are provided when possible. I regret that I am only able to include such a small percentage of the total diversity in this book. The majority of moths on these pages were attracted to the light on our veranda in Grand Case.

The last page of this section is devoted to some commonly seen moth caterpillars.

Melipotis januaris is fairly large, quite common and attracted to lights at night. The male is pictured, the female is similar, but slightly more drab.

The tobacco budworm, *Heliothis virescens*, is considered a major pest in many areas. The caterpillars feed on tobacco, cotton and soybean plants.

This noctuid (*Dyomyx* sp.) may be *Dyomyx jugator*, a species endemic to the Lesser Antilles, and is quite common on the island.

Phyprosopus tristriga is a noctuid that is endemic to the Antilles.

Isogona scindens is a noctuid found from the southern United States, through the Caribbean and northern South America.

The omatochila moth (*Ommatochila mundula*) is a small noctuid that ranges from the southern parts of the US to Central America and the Caribbean.

The striped grass looper (*Mocis repanda*) is found in Central America and the Caribbean. Its grass-eating caterpillars are considered a pest to corn and sugar cane.

This noctuid is probably *Elaphria agrotina*, but variations in the color of this species make precise identification difficult.

This brown leaf mimic (*Metallata absumens*) was found on leaf litter in the forest on Pic Paradis. To complete the illusion of being a leaf, when approached it flutters quickly only a foot or two away like a leaf blown in the wind.

Spodoptera latifascia has many common names. My favorite is velvet armyworm. This large Noctuid is quite common on the island, as is its caterpillar.

Another variation on the leaf mimic, the velvetbean moth (*Anticarsia gemmatalis*) was also found on the forest floor on Pic Paradis. The caterpillar of this moth is a pest of several bean crops.

Semiothisa everiata is quite variable in color, although the basic pattern remains the same. In some cases the outermost band of the wings is darker than in this individual.

This unobtrusive geometrid is probably the soft-lined wave (*Scopula inductata*), although there are several similar species in this genus. It was photographed on Pinel islet during the day.

Synchlora cupedinaria is small, but beautifully colored in green and pink. There are multiple subspecies in the Caribbean.

This small moth is a regular visitor and is possibly a geometrid from the genus *Eumacrodes*.

The southern emerald moth (*Synchlora frondaria*) can be distinguished from similar moths by the white line running down its abdomen.

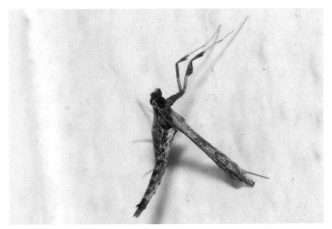

This peculiar looking moth is likely from the family Pterophoridae, the plume moths.

This strikingly beautiful moth is a pyralid (superfamily Pyraloidea), from the family Crambidae, possibly genus *Synclera*. It was seen resting during the day in a mountain forest.

Palpita isoscelalis has translucent wings and was seen in the forest on Pic Paradis. A number of similar species from this genus are found in the Americas.

Another striking pyralid, this beet webworm (*Spoladea recurvalis*) was found at night. The caterpillars of this species feed on beets and other agricultural crops.

The melonworm (*Diaphania hyalinata*) is a rather striking pyralid that has two large hairpencils (scent brushes) at the end of its abdomen that it waves in the air while resting.

Eulepte gastralis is a pyralid found in the Caribbean, Central America and South America.

The white-roped glaphyria (*Glaphyria sequistrialis*) is a small, but brightly-colored moth that often visits our lights at night.

This pyralid is probably *Leucania subpunctata*, but analysis of the moth's genitalia would be necessary to determine this with certainty.

This tiny and peculiar moth was found in a field in Grand Case. It is a cosmet moth (family Cosmopterigidae), possibly from the awesomely-named genus *Cosmopterix*.

Achyra bifidalis is known to be a pest of cotton plants and is a member of the large and diverse moth superfamily Pyraloidea.

Dichogama redtenbacheri is a fairly common pyralid on St. Martin. While the shape of the markings is consistent, in some individuals they are obscured by a dark orange covering most of the wings.

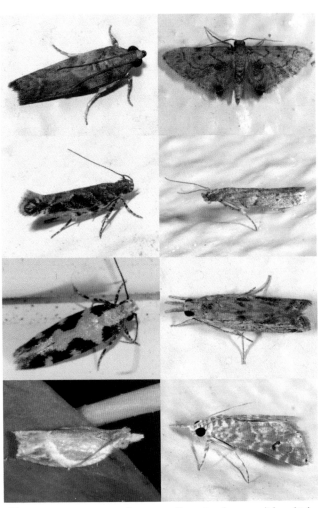

There are many types of very small moth, often pyralids, which may be found at lights. I have found them very difficult to identify, even when they have distinctive coloration. The moth on the bottom right is *Hellula rogatalis*.

Also referred to as the garden armyworm or lateral lined armyworm, the caterpillar of *Spodoptera latifascia* eats a variety of plants including garden crops.

This large caterpillar, likely a sphinx moth, was writhing in the street and died shortly afterward. In retrospect, it was likely the victim of parasitism, but at the time I did not think to dissect it.

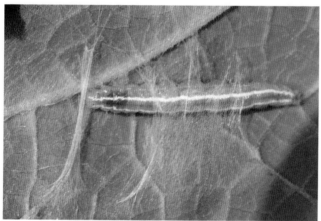

Like many caterpillars, the melonworm (*Diaphania hyalinata*) uses silk to fold or roll the edge of the leaf into a shelter where it will pupate.

Caterpillars of geometrid moths are often referred to as inchworms due to their looping gait.

The caterpillar of the rustic sphinx (*Manduca rustica*) is quite large and very beautiful. It is very similar in appearance to the closely-related tobacco hornworm.

Larvae of bagworm moths (family Psychidae) create protective cases from silk and organic matter. These cases are common on building walls where they have attached to pupate.

COLEOPTERA

Despite the abundance of avid coleopterists, this order poses a significant taxonomical challenge due to the large number of species, often estimated at over one million, with over 400,000 currently described.

The beetles of St. Martin are quite varied and only small minority of species are included in this guide. Given the relative lack of research, it would not be surprising if there were undiscovered, possibly endemic, species on the island.

Trachyderes succinctus is a longhorn beetle from the family Cerambycidae, a large group of beetles containing over 20,000 known species.

This relatively nondescript scarab is probably from either the Dynastinae subfamily or Aphodiinae subfamily. Identification in this family may require analysis of the antennae, claws and mouthparts. Like several other species, it was attracted to lights at night.

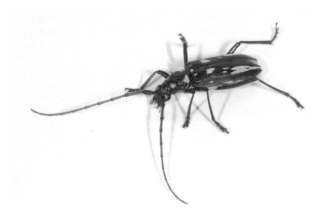

Eburia decemmaculata is perhaps the most common cerambycid on the island, and I have seen them both in the daytime and at night.

The gazelle scarab (*Onthophagus gazella*) is also known as the brown dung beetle. I have noticed individuals of this species that were heavily infested with tiny mites (see Other Invertebrates).

This cerambycid, seen on Pic Paradis, is probably *Solenoptera chalumeaui*, a species named in 1979 based on specimens from Saint Martin.

This very unusual cerambycid is probably from the tribe Necydalini in the subfamily Lepturinae. Its elytra (wing covers) are very short compared to its body. Some members of this group imitate wasps.

A click-beetle, family Elateridae, was attracted to an outdoor light at night. Members of this family have a spine and notch on their underside which can be used to spring them into the air.

This small firefly (family Lampyridae) is probably from the genus *Photuris*, but a similar specimen from the Harvard Museum of Comparative Zoology online database is as yet unidentified.

Darkling beetles, family Tenebrio, are typically found beneath logs and stones, but are sometimes attracted to lights at night. They primarily feed on fresh or decaying plant matter.

Aspisoma maculatum is a much larger species from the firefly family from the subfamily Photininae. This pair was seen mating during the day on a roadside plant.

The vedalia beetle (*Rodolia cardinalis*) is an Austrailian species first introduced into the new world in California in 1888 as a natural pest control agent. It is a member of the ladybug family (Coccinellidae).

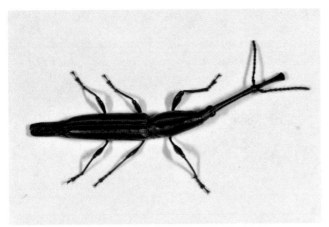

Brentid weevils, family Brentidae, are primarily tropical, highly elongated weevils. This specimen was found in the undergrowth of a montane forest.

The southern golden tortoise beetle (*Charidotella sexpunctata*) are primarily found on plants from the morning glory family (Convolvulaceae).

With over 60,000 species in several families, weevils (superfamily Curculionoidea) are difficult to identify. This one is from the subfamily Entiminae, the broad-nosed weevils and may be *Polydrusus* sp.

Chelymorpha cribraria is another colorful tortoise beetle. When attacked by predators such as ants, they clamp down on the leaf where they are standing and they are protected by their shield-like exoskeleton.

This very small weevil is from the family Curculioninae, the true weevils, and may be *Anthonomus* sp. Many weevils are agricultural pests, and some species on the island also infest dry goods like flour and pasta.

Chalepus sanguinicolis is from the same family as the tortoise beetles, Chrysomelidae.

This chrysomelid is *Cryptocephalus* sp., possibly *baleatus*. The genus name refers to the fact that the head is somewhat hidden by the thorax. They are often seen near lights at night.

Disonycha spilotrachela is a flea beetle (tribe Alticini). They can be seen in grassy areas by day or at lights at night.

There are, of course, many other beetles from the family Chrysomelidae. Many of them are colorful, and most of them are quite small.

This mating pair of flea beetles may be *Altica occidentalis*, or perhaps one of the 300 other species in that genus.

There are several species of aquatic beetle (family Dytiscidae) documented on Saint Martin. They live in freshwater habitats and are typically black or very dark brown. A small bubble of air they carry with them gives their underside a silvery appearance.

HYMENOPTERA

The order Hymenoptera includes ants, bees and wasps. While many species are solitary, this order includes the majority of social insects, many of which have complex colony structures and highly-differentiated castes performing distinct roles in the colony.

This group also includes some of the more dangerous insects on the island. Inadvertently stepping on a fire ant mound may bring the wrath of thousands of ants, while any overhang or branch may harbor a paper wasp nest which will be defended if one accidentally gets too close.

This group of ants is tending leafhopper nymphs in exchange for sweet nectar they excrete. I have also seen ants on the island tending aphids and scale insects.

The inside of an ant colony reveals pupae of multiple sizes. In some species, there are multiple castes of workers perform specialized tasks. The larger pupae may also be males and females who fly off to form new colonies.

Winged male and female ants occasionally swarm at dusk, sometimes in astounding numbers. After mating, the males die and the females become the queen of a new colony.

While many ants are scavengers, in this case a group of ants are attacking a live caterpillar.

Ants are exceedingly common and sometimes a pest, but they also offer the valuable service of carting away organic debris, in this case a dead termite.

This swarm of honeybees (*Apis* sp.) has probably recently split from a hive with the old queen following the birth of new queens and has not yet found a suitable location for a new hive.

Over a dozen of these ichneumon wasps (*Ophion* sp.) were seen hanging from a tree in the forest, possibly because they had all recently hatched from the same host insect.

Large, black carpenter bees (*Xylocopa* sp.) are commonly seen feeding at beach morning glory and other flowers.

This scoliid wasp, probably *Campsomeris trifasciata* feeds on pollen, although some members of the family Scoliidae feed on beetle larvae.

This large bee, probably also *Xylocopa* sp., I have seen swarming near the beach frequently. While they don't seem to feed, pairs or small groups seem to fight, although perhaps they are courting.

This sand wasp (*Stictia signata*) is seen emerging from the underground chamber where its larvae grow, feeding on insect prey that has been left for them.

The ensign wasp (*Evania appendigaster*) is a parasitic wasp. Eggs are laid in the oothecae (egg cases) of cockroaches, where the larvae develop. When walking, this wasp tends to bob its abdomen up and down.

Mud daubers (*Sceliphron caementarium*) construct mud nests during the rainy season, often on the sides of abandoned buildings.

A group of spider wasps (probably *Prionyx thomae*) may have been newly hatched from their host as this is typically a solitary species.

The jack Spaniard (*Mischocyttarus mexicanus cubicola*) is an exceedingly common wasp which builds paper nests on trees, on buildings and in rock caves.

This small wasp with an unusual tapered abdomen was found feeding from flowers near the beach.

A closer look at a jack Spaniard nest reveals the larvae inside.. They commonly on buildings and other man made structures and readily defend their nests. Their sting is painful, but subsides quickly.

NEUROPTERA

The lace-winged insects are named for the visible veins in their transparent wings. Although they look very different, their closest living relatives are the beetles. This order is primarily predatory, usually feeding on small insects, and has distinct larval, pupal and adult stages. They are easily attracted to lights at night, probably due to the presence of small insects that they can feed upon.

Unrelated to the praying mantis, the mantisfly (*Hispinae* sp.) is an example of convergent evolution, a process by which unrelated organisms develop a similar biological trait.

Green lacewings, family Chrysopidae, feed on small insects such as aphids, and are frequently used as pest control agents. Their tiny eggs are laid on delicate stalks on the underside of leaves.

Antlions, from the family Myrmeleontidae have clubbed antennae and superficially resemble dragonflies.

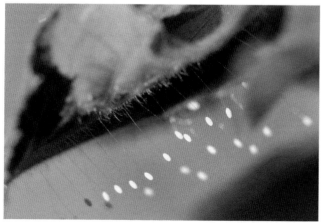

Lacewings lay their eggs on slender stalks, usually on the underside of leaves. Their larvae, like the adults, feed primarily on aphids.

Cone-shaped traps in sand or loose dirt are made by antlion larvae who wait at the bottom for small insects to fall into them. They are easily seen all over the island.

DIPTERA

This order includes many of the most annoying insects on the island, including flies, mosquitoes and gnats. On St. Martin mosquitoes, specifically *Aedes aegypti*, represent a significant health hazard, transmitting dengue fever, an often severe tropical disease.

Dipterans use one pair of wings to propel themselves in flight, while the other pair has been modified into tiny, knobbed structures known as halteres which function as accelerometers to increase stability in flight. This adaptation gives flies in particular the ability to perform amazing aerial acrobatics.

The white stripes on the legs of this mosquito may indicate that it is the dengue-carrying *Aedes aegypti*.

DENGUE FEVER

Dengue fever is a tropical disease caused by a group of viruses that is typically transmitted to humans by mosquitoes. The severity of the disease is variable, ranging from flu-like symptoms lasting for several days to a hemorrhagic fever that can be near-fatal and typically requires hospitalization.

Symptoms generally include fever and severe muscle and joint pain that has earned it the name bonebreak fever. Pain behind the eyes is a distinctive symptom of this disease. Other symptoms may include rashes, vomiting, nausea and diarrhea. Hemorrhagic dengue may cause bleeding, both internally and externally and is accompanied by a severe drop in platelet count.

There is currently no vaccine for this disease. Treatment typically involves maintaining hydration and platelet infusions if necessary. The use of mosquito repellent can decrease the likelihood of infection. In St. Martin, insecticide spraying near urban areas is done on occasion, but unfortunately, this is detrimental to a variety of insect species as well as other animals.

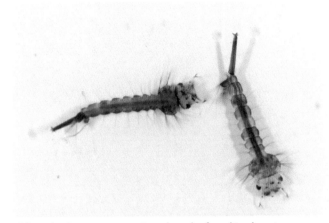

Mosquito larvae are aquatic and can be found in almost any open source of fresh water. In this photo they are significantly magnified, thank goodness.

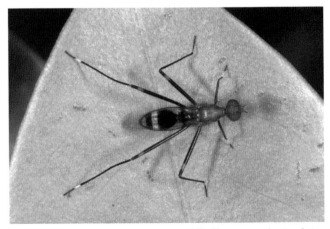

I was quite perplexed by this unusual fly, *Taeniaptera lasciva*. It is a member of the Micropezidae, a family with unusually long legs. Many species in this family mimic ants or wasps.

This elongated syrphid fly (probably *Xylota* sp.), like many in this family, has evolved to resemble bees and wasps.

This blowfly (family Calliphoridae, possibly *Chrysomya megacephala*) is drinking a droplet of water from a small tree branch.

The syrphid fly, also known as the flower fly or hoverfly, feed primarily on pollen and nectar and often resemble bees. This specimen is probably *Palpada vinetorum*.

This small Lauxaniid is probably *Poecilominettia* sp., possibly *valida*. I normally see them at night, which his unusual for a fly.

This odd looking fly is a dance fly (family Hybotidae). Some members of this family crawl in distinctive patterns when hunting for food, which gave rise to their common name.

These large gray and black flesh flies (family Sarcophagidae) are making sweet love on the underside of a branch. The larvae typically live in carrion.

HEMIPTERA

Members of this order is often referred to as true bugs, and it also includes aphids, cicadas, planthoppers and leafhoppers. Their defining characteristic is the straw-like proboscis that they use to pierce and suck liquid from their food source, which is typically plants. They have an incomplete metamorphosis, growing from egg to nymph to adult without pupating. The nymph stage tends to somewhat resemble the adult.

These planthoppers (*Ormenaria rufifascia*) are also related to cicadas and leafhoppers. They feed on the sap of various plants, including palm trees.

This cicada, possibly *Proarna* sp., is more often seen than heard. Cicadas are from the superfamily Cicadoidea and live underground as nymphs, often for several years, before emerging as adults. (Photo M.A.)

Leptoglossus balteatus is a leaf-footed bug (family Coreidae). They are named after the leaf-like portion of its rear legs. When approached, they give off a very strong, but not unpleasant odor.

Leafhoppers (family Cicadellidae) are a diverse group including over 20,000 species. They are generally quite small and often resemble cidadas, to which they are closely related.

The St. Andrew's cotton stainer (*Dysdercus andreae*) is a brightly-colored, quite common resident of the island and is found throughout the West Indies either on living plants or decaying leaves. Inset, top left: the nymph (immature) of this species.

The milkweed assassin bug (*Zelus longipes*) has similar coloration to the cotton-stainer, but very different habits. Assassin bugs (Reduviidae) are predatory, injecting their prey with saliva that liquefies their tissues, which are then sucked out.

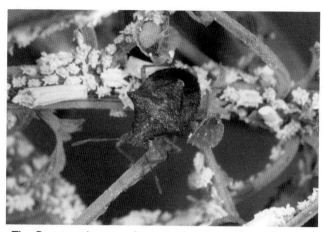

The Pentatomidae are often shield-shaped and include stink-bugs, although many other species of hemipteran produce strong odors as a defense mechanism.

The life cycle of the milkweed assassin bug. Clockwise from top left: newly hatched nymphs emerging from a line of eggs on the bottom of the branch, an older nymph, the empty exoskeleton of a larger nymph, the adult.

A porch light left on at night invariably attracts a variety of small hemipterans.

An alydid, possibly *Megalotomus* sp., probably one of a number of species from the family Alydidae on the island.

There are a number of aquatic hemipterans, such as this water boatman, which is either *Trichocorixa reticulata* or *T. verticalis*. This individual was photographed during a swarm when hundreds landed on our balcony at night.

ORTHOPTERA

This order of insects includes most of the noisemaking arthropods on the island, with many species that chirp or sing to attract mates. The order is quite varied on the island and includes diurnal and nocturnal species that inhabit pretty much every type of habitat on the island from the coasts to the highest peaks.

While most grasshoppers are active during the day, many crickets and katydids are more active at night and spend their days hiding under rocks and logs or in the undergrowth.

This true grasshopper from the family Acrididae is much smaller than the *Schistocera* that are also found on the island.

A locust (*Schistocerca* sp., possibly *pallens*) is quite common on the island, found in most grassy and shrub areas. This genus is found in many parts of the world and is famous for swarming.

Alternately referred to as a conocephaline katydid or coneheaded grasshopper (*Neoconocephalus* sp., possibly *triops*), this species is seasonally quite common at lights at night. I have also seen a brown version, either a similar species or a color variant.

A nymph (juvenile) locust (*Schistocerca* sp.) looks very different from the adult, but does share many of the same facial features. Locust is a term for grasshoppers that have a tendency to swarm when conditions are right.

This peculiar katydid (*Nesonotus* sp.) was found near the top of Pic Paradis.

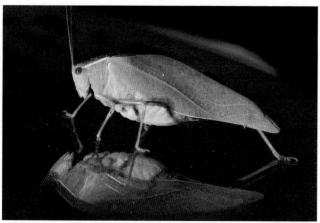

The katydid family (Tettigoniidae) is quite diverse in the Caribbean, including many species that imitate leaves as a form of camouflage.

This arboreal cricket (possibly subfamily Eneopterinae) was found in a tree in the Bell Point area.

A juvenile katydid, possibly *Phoebolampta caeruleotergum*, a species discovered on St. Martin in 2008.

Cave crickets (*Amphiacusta* spp.) may also be found under rocks and in leaf litter.

My best guess is that this is a winged bush cricket (family Trigoniidinae), possibly *Cyrtoxipha* sp. It was seen on the side of a building at night.

The mole cricket (family Gryllotalpidae), is a rarely-seen nocturnal cricket that spends its days in often extensive underground tunnel systems.

ODONATA

This order includes dragonflies and their daintier cousins the damselflies. These insects are the last remaining members of a lineage that extends back over 300 million years. These adept fliers begin their life as predatory aquatic larvae that are able to live in brackish waters, which may help them prosper on St. Martin where there is a relative lack of freshwater bodies.

Aside from their relative size, an easy way to distinguish between dragonflies (Anisoptera) and damselflies (Zygoptera) is that dragonflies keep their wings spread when at rest, while damselflies fold them above their backs.

Red dragonfly, possibly *Brachymesia* sp. seen near a roadside ditch that is seasonally filled with fresh water.

Rambur's forktail (*Ischnura ramburii*) is the most common species of damselfly in the Americas. The male can be identified by the completely blue segment near the end of the abdomen.

Several species of dragonfly have banded wings like this specimen, possibly the band-winged dragonlet (*Erytrhodiplax umbrata*). This species exhibits sexual dimorphism, and females do not have dark bands on their wings.

The great pondhawk (*Erythemis vesiculosa*) is large and brilliantly green. It is a widespread species from North America to South America.

OTHER INSECTS

Several orders of insect are represented on the island by either fewer or less conspicuous varieties. Among those collected here are the silverfish (Thysanura), cockroaches (Blattaria), walking stick (Phasmatodea), earwig (Dermaptera) and termites (Isoptera).

It is also likely that praying mantises (Mantodea) are present on the island, although I have yet to see them myself.

Cockroaches, clockwise from top left: American cockroach (*Periplaneta americana*) adult (locally called the mahogany bird), American cockroach nymph, flightless cockroach (probably *Hemiblabera* sp.), small arboreal cockroach (family Blattellidae).

Silverfish are primitive insects typically found in rotting leaves and other detritus on the forest floor.

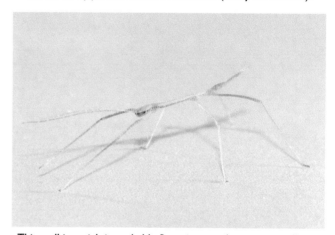

This walking stick is probably *Bacteria* sp. and given its small size is most likely a nymph. It was found at night in Grand Case and waves its body back and forth to look like it is swaying in the wind.

Termite colonies may be found in rotting logs. Winged termites sent out to create new colonies are also attracted to lights at night. Similarities between termites and some cockroaches have prompted some scientists to group them together.

Earwigs (order Dermaptera) are nocturnal insects that feed on both plants and small insects. This one flew onto our table while dining outdoors. Its large hindwings are folded beneath the short, leathery forewings which serve as wing covers.

The brown widow (*Latrodectus geometricus*), a cousin of the infamous black widow, rests inside a silken pouch. The venom of this spider is of comparable toxicity to that of the black widow, but the bite is typically not painful, perhaps because little or no venom is injected.

SPIDERS

After the insects, spiders (belonging to the arachnid order Araneae) are probably the most varied group of animals on the island. I would guess that the number of species is in the dozens, but to my knowledge, a formal survey of spider diversity on the island has not yet been done.

The spiders of St. Martin have a wide diversity of hunting techniques and seem to occupy almost every type of habitat on the island, from scrubland to dense forest to human habitations.

The most visible species are included here in some detail, while other species are included with photographs and identification where available. Future field research on St. Martin has been planned and will hopefully shed additional light on the spider diversity of the island.

The brown widow can easily be identified by the presence of its distinctive egg sac, a spiky ball made of silk. Locally, the brown widow is often referred to as the black widow due to the resemblance.

SILVER ARGIOPE (*Argiope argentata*) AND BANDED GARDEN SPIDER (*Argiope trifasciata*)

The silver argiope is very common on St. Martin. In scrubland areas, it can be almost impossible to walk between any two nearby bushes without walking through one of their webs. The upperside of this spider is silvery white in front and dark with white markings in back. The underside is dark with yellow markings, and the legs are typically banded in black, yellow and orange.

An orb-weaving spider of the family Araneidae, it weaves large webs, sometimes reinforcing the center with an x-shaped group of zig-zagging lines. Young individuals may weave webs in grass with irregular reinforcement in the center. I have also seen smaller individuals in webs created at the edge of larger webs.

When approached, they typically run towards one of the anchor points of their web. The females can be quite large, over three centimeters in body-length, while the males don't exceed two centimeters. The bite of this spider is reported as being painful and itchy for an hour or so, but despite walking through hundreds of webs I have not yet been bitten.

The banded garden spider is a closely related species, similar in most respects, but the top of its abdomen is banded. It is widely distributed around the world, but much less common on St. Martin than the silver argiope.

The silver argiope is typically seen in the center of their large web. In this case, it has recently caught a great southern white.

While most webs seem to lack the distinctive x-shaped reinforcement, it may be present or partially present on some silver argiope webs.

Aside from its banded abdomen, the banded garden spider closely resembles the more common silver argiope. The top view is on the left and the bottom view on the right. The underside features two yellow lines on either side of two pairs of small white dots.

A detail of the underside of the silver argiope shows a thick yellow band on a mostly black abdomen.

SPINY-BACKED ORBWEAVER (*Gasteracantha cancriformis*)

This spider, also referred to as the crab spider and many other combinations of crab, spiny and orbweaver, is quite common on the island and inhabits both scrubland and forested areas. It is also quite variable in color and markings.

This spider is normally identified by the presence of six spines on the abdomen, but on St. Martin typically only four are visible. There are a variety of different color variations, the most common being red-orange and yellow or black and white. In North America, which makes up the bulk of its range, there are also a variety of color variations, but typically all six spines are visible.

Although its webs are quite large, the spider itself is small, less than a centimeter in length. These spiders typically live only shortly after reproducing. Males of this species are much smaller than females. One may easily identify their webs because the outer support lines are reinforced at regular intervals, giving the appearance of a dotted line along the perimeter of the web.

A typical red and white specimen. This is probably the most common color variant on the island.

Black with white spots is a relatively less common color variant. The large differences in color and pattern are quite striking for a single species.

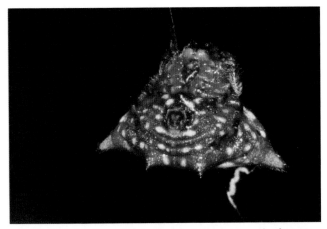

The underside of a red and yellow individual shows the four visible spikes and a typical pattern of yellow spots on a red background.

Black with a white, cream or yellow back is a relatively common variant on the island, and similar in pattern to the yellow and red variant.

GRAY WALL JUMPER (*Menemerus bivittatus*) AND PANTROPICAL WALL JUMPER (*Plexippus paykulli*)

These jumping spiders, particularly the gray wall jumper, are exceedingly common around human habitation, and I typically have at least a dozen in and around my apartment at any given time. These spiders do not spin webs, but feed by attacking their prey on foot. In most cases, they are not particularly bothered by human presence, and this is particularly true when they are devouring a fresh kill.

If food is scarce, cannibalism is an option for the gray wall jumper, particularly if you are a large female. The four large, front-facing eyes are seen clearly. Additional eyes are on the sides of the head for a wider field of view.

The male pantropical wall jumper has a brown and white striped abdomen which features a light stripe down the middle, essentially the opposite pattern from the male gray wall jumper.

The male gray wall jumper is a light brown with a dark stripe running down the abdomen.

The female pantropical jumper, seen here with a freshly-caught fly, is generally a darker brown with some lighter markings on the top of the abdomen.

The female gray wall jumper is essentially the opposite of her male counterpart, light brown with dark stripes running down either side of the abdomen.

ADDITIONAL SPIDERS

The admittedly incomplete selection of spiders on the following pages is meant to serve as a starting point for understanding the tremendous variety and great beauty of these creatures.

It may be worth noting that many totally unrelated spiders are referred to as crab spiders because they either look or walk like crabs. Conversely, various crabs are referred to as spider crabs. There is no taxonomic significance to these common names.

Jumping spiders (family Salticidae) are quite acrobatic and sometimes very colorful. This one was waving its white pedipalps, perhaps in an attempt to attract prey.

Thomisidae are called crab spiders based on their appearance. They typically sit on plants and ambush their prey. This particular species is colored to match the flowers where it lies in wait.

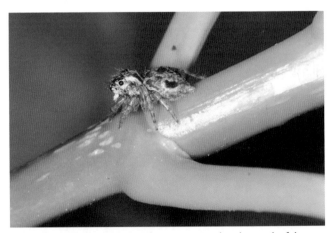

Another jumping spider, with an intricate, but less colorful pattern. Their excellent eyesight includes four types of color receptors, allowing them to process a wider spectrum of light.

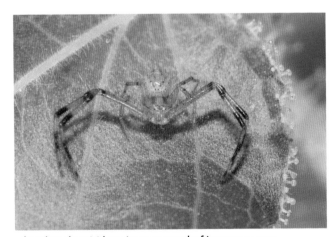

Another thomisid awaits prey on a leaf in a grassy area.

In this jumper, the large anterior median eyes (i.e., middle front eyes) are clearly visible, which is a distinguishing feature of this family and crucial to their hunting ability.

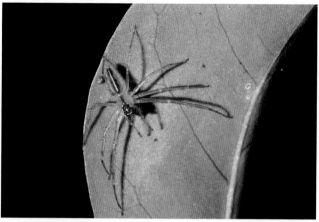

This green jumper (*Lyssomanes* sp.) is quite similar in body shape to the lynx spiders (Oxyopidae), but the large anterior median eyes identify it as a salticid.

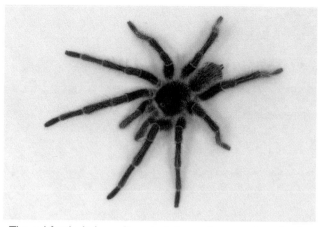

The subfamily Ischnocolinae includes various species of relatively small, fast-moving tarantulas like this one (*Holothele* sp.). Although the leg-span of this individual was over 10cm when spread, it often folded its legs over itself to protect its body.

The lynx spider *Oxyopes salticus* has eyes arranged in a hexagon pattern and spikes on its legs, traits it shares with other Oxyopids.

This ground-dwelling spider (family Barychelidae) is a very small type of tarantula, usually 2-3 cm in length. It is usually found under logs or stones during the day, although many species climb trees at night to hunt.

It is always a treat to see a cluster of spiderlings (baby spiders). Depending on the species, the mother may protect the egg case, or even carry the young on her back.

This wall crab spider (family Selenopidae) is quite common under rocks and logs during the day. At night they may be seen climbing on walls.

This dew-drop spider (*Argyrodes elevatus*) is a kleptoparasite, living at the edge of larger orb-weaving spiders and stealing their prey.

This large and rather striking araneid, perhaps of genus *Neoscona*, does not seem to be particularly common on the island. I have only seen it once or twice.

I found this recently deceased spider still clinging to a bush. It is likely from the family Sparassidae, known as the huntsman spiders or giant crab spiders.

This orb weaver (*Leucauge* sp., possibly *regnyi*) is primarily found in mountain forests, where it can be quite common.

Seen on my wall at night, this spider is likely a sparassid as well. Although smaller than most tarantulas, sparassids can be quite large, but they are typically not regarded as dangerous.

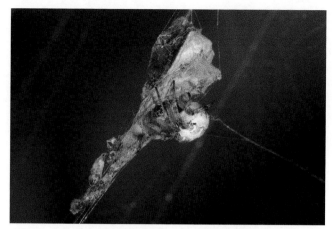

This spider, probably of the genus *Metepeira*, creates a retreat in its web by weaving leaves and other debris together.

This orb-weaver (family Araneidae) was guarding her egg sac. Along with most of the other spiders on this page, I found her at the abandoned ruins of La Belle Creole resort.

The tropical spitting spider (*Scytodes longipes*) captures its prey by spitting a sticky and poisonous venom, which immobilizes its prey.

This spider, probably an oxyopid, or lynx spider, was also seen at La Belle Creole. It would seem that human architecture in the absence of humans offers a very desirable environment for spiders.

This extremely dainty member of family Pholcidae, which are often referred to as daddy long legs, was found in our home.

The Caribbean hermit crab (*Coenobita clypeatus*) is very common, and can be found from the seaside to the mountains. Primarily nocturnal, they can be seen traveling during the day or hiding beneath stones, sometimes in large groups. This crab is wearing the shell of the East African land snail, a recent invasive species. Historically they utilized much sturdier shells from marine snails.

CRUSTACEANS

As far as I can tell, there are only a handful of non-marine crustaceans on the island, although some species are quite common. Most species are present throughout the Caribbean.

When hiking in the hills, the sound of falling pebbles is usually made by the Caribbean hermit crab (*Coenobita clypeatus*) retracting into its shell, falling from wherever it was walking. These colorful crabs have gills rather than lungs, but are still able to respire using the humidity of the air and water kept inside their shell. They are also skilled climbers, able to climb trees and rocky cliffs.

Large burrows in the sand or dirt, often near the coast or salt ponds, are usually the homes of the great land crab (*Cardisoma guanhumi*), a common species that grows quite large over the course of up to 30 molting cycles.

At the edge of mangroves wetlands, fiddler crabs (*Uca pugnax*) are quite abundant. Easily identified by their one grossly oversized claw, they typically retreat into the water or into burrows in sand or mud near the shore when approached.

The ghost crab (*Ocypode quadrata*) gets its name from its translucent shell and can be seen scurrying around sandy beaches amongst the waves where it feeds.

The mangrove crab (*Aratus pisonii*) and black land crab (*Gecarcinus ruricola*) are less frequently seen in the open, but often have burrows under rocks or logs where they rest during the day. The black land crab is known locally as the jumbie crab. Jumbies are spirits of the dead and typically considered evil, so this crab is not eaten.

The black land crab (*Gecarcinus ruricola*) is a small land crab which spends its larval stage in the ocean before returning to land where they may be found in burrows under stones.

The fiddler crab (*Uca pugnax*) is common near the shore of salt ponds and mangrove wetlands. The single large claw may sometimes be as large as the rest of the body.

The mangrove crab (*Aratus pisonii*) is found near mangroves and is semi-aquatic.

The ghost crab (*Ocypode quadrata*) has a translucent shell and is primarily seen on sandy beaches where it feeds on organic matter brought in by waves.

The great land crab (*Cardisoma guanhumi*) is often pale gray or tan and is most frequently seen peeking out of large burrows in the sand or dirt. Large adults may weigh up to 500 grams. This crab is locally known as the bush crab.

The Caribbean hermit crab is also known as the purple pincher, after the large purple claw it uses to block the entrance to its shell. Others call it the soldier crab.

The tailless whipscorpion or whip spider (*Phrynus goesii*) is a nocturnal arachnid that may be found beneath stones or logs during the day. Despite their appearance, they are harmless and have no venom. They feed on insects and other small invertebrates.

OTHER ARTHROPODS

The remainder of arthropod species are collected here for convenience, and include members of several classes: Arachnida (the whip spider), Chilapoda (centipedes) and Diplopoda (millipedes). Many of these creatures are nocturnal and may go unnoticed by many visitors. Other species documented on the island but not pictured here include one species of scorpion and several species of mite.

It is possible that one or more species of velvet worm exists on the island. These curious creatures share attributes with both arthropods and annelids (segmented worms) and are classified under their own phylum, Onychophora. Notoriously reclusive, if they are present it is probably in damp, forested mountain areas.

Despite their appearance, whip spiders are quite harmless, unless you are a small insect.

Due to space constraints, terrestrial isopods have been included here, although they are crustaceans.

The giant centipede (*Scolopendra* sp.) may reach over 20 cm in length and is capable of delivering a painful bite. They are locally used in a rum flavored by their venom.

Terrestrial isopods, often called woodlice, sow bugs or pill bugs, are primitive crustaceans with many body segments. They are typically nocturnal and primarily feed on dead plant matter.

This red rhinocricid millipede is quite common on the island and may be found traveling on the ground, particularly at night. They are locally known as rain worms because they are active when it rains.

This spider-like creature is a sun spider from the arachnid order Solifugae. While some species from this family get quite large they are generally harmless and feed primarily on termites and other small invertebrates.

Polydesmid millipedes typically have a flattened body of about 20 segments and can produce hydrogen cyanide to discourage predators.

There are a number of mite (subclass Acari) species on the island, at least two of which seem to be attached to this scarab. The smaller ones resemble genus *Poecilochirus*, which hitch rides on beetles to carrion sources where they eat fly eggs and larvae.

The East African land snail (*Achatina fulica*) is an invasive species that is a serious agricultural pest. The extent of its impact on the natural environment of St. Martin is unknown, but it is extremely common on the island. They are quite large, often several inches in length.

MOLLUSKS

While undoubtedly less diverse than their marine counterparts in the surrounding waters, the terrestrial mollusks of St. Martin are varied and often beautiful. Despite the lack of cloud forest and irregular rainfall, at least 47 species have been documented on the island, representing several families.

Unfortunately, the largest and most visible snail is a highly invasive African species. Its impact on native snail populations is as yet unmeasured, but can't be good, and eradication seems highly unlikely.

Early collectors of non-marine mollusks on the island in the 1800s included several French naval officers, a Danish apothecary, a French priest, a Swedish geologist and a physician from Wisconsin. Unfortunately, many of their collections have been lost over the years.

Zachrysia provisoria is from the family Camaenidae, a diverse group with many species in the Caribbean. This snail was found in the damp hollow of a tree stump, surrounded by decomposing leaves.

A snail from the family Helicinidae. These small, often brightly colored snails are found in moist mountain forests. Though similar in appearance, they are not closely related to other land snails.

Snails from the family Bulimidae are quite diverse in the Caribbean. On the left is the West Indian bulimulus (*Bulimulus guadalupensis*), and on the right is *Drymaeus elongatus*.

This immature orthalicid, possibly *Orthalicus princeps*, was found feeding on vegetation in Quartier d'Orleans.

This diminutive snail is a subulimid, probably *Opeas* sp., which is typically found under boards or rotting logs. They are sometimes known as awlsnails because of their long, skinny shape.

This small annulariid is likely from the genus *Chondropoma*, which has several species documented on the island.

The Caribbean leatherleaf (*Sarasinula plebeia*) from the family Veronicellidae is found primarily in moist highland forest. It is considered an agricultural pest.

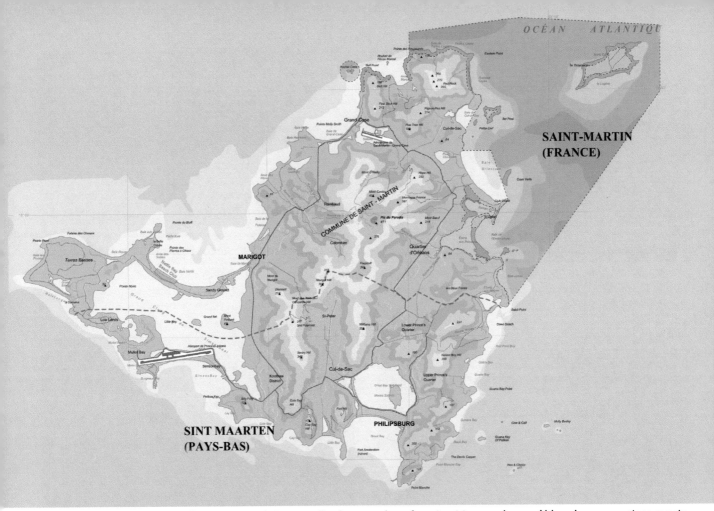

Saint Martin is home to a rapidly growing population as well as large number of tourist visitors each year. Although some portions remain undeveloped, the strain imposed by humans on the local environment is readily apparent. Still, there are many areas where the beauty of the natural landscape and its inhabitants can be enjoyed.

NOTES ON CONSERVATION AND SELECTED AREAS OF INTEREST

On the following pages I have chosen to highlight a few selected areas of interest that represent some of the major types of habitat on St. Martin. Before I do so, it is necessary to mention that every part of the island has suffered from destructive human involvement.

During colonial times, nearly all of the natural vegetation was destroyed for agriculture, and it can be assumed that all or nearly all the existing forest on in the central mountains and elsewhere is secondary growth. Although the Wilderness area at the northeast tip of the island remains undeveloped, the presence of introduced mongoose has severely impacted reptile populations. Most undeveloped lowland and hill areas have been radically transformed by grazing cattle and goats. Even the uninhabited offshore islands are home to invasive species including rats, mice and goats.

In more recent times, massive population growth and the development of a large tourism industry has put additional strain on the island. As late as the 1960s the population of the island was estimated to be around 5,000 people. Today, it is close to 80,000, with an estimated one million or more tourists per year. Every salt pond and mangrove wetland on the island is polluted and the largest cave on the island was filled in during development in the 1990s. A large area on Hope Hill is currently being mined for building materials, while new resorts and an expanded airport have been expanding into the lagoon and nearby mangroves. Near Baie Longue, an overloaded waste treatment center discharges raw sewage into the sea a few hundred meters offshore.

Development takes place with little or no consideration for the environmental impact, and the budget does not seem to exist to handle refuse and sewage for an increased population. These factors do not bode well for the survival of the delicate ecosystems on the island.

There are, however, some bright spots in this otherwise gloomy picture. The French Reserve Naturelle de Saint Martin has set aside significant marine and terrestrial areas as a nature reserve. On the Dutch side, the Nature Foundation St. Maarten has established the St. Maarten Marine Park, which includes several islets that serve as breeding grounds for marine birds, and is hoping to establish a terrestrial park at some time in the future. A private business, Loterie Farm, maintains 135 acres on Pic Paradis as a private reserve and eco-tourism center. Through a combination of efforts, perhaps it will be possible to slow the destruction of St. Martin's natural heritage.

Mining for construction materials and the associated roads have permanently scarred the face of Hope Hill. During heavy rains, topsoil erosion from this area is clearly visible.

A green heron hunts in a trash filled canal. After being opened to connect the pond to the sea, the nearby bay filled with algae blooms within two weeks.

The line between forest and goat pasture is often stark, as seen on this hill.

Unfortunately, the wetlands of the island are a dumping ground for visible trash as well as sewage and other forms of pollution.

Coastal areas of the island are largely developed, although on the French side such development is on a much smaller scale.

In this view of the hills leading out to Bell Point, a cattle shelter can be seen in the foreground. The scrub area serves as pasture for the cattle, while the top of the hills is covered with secondary forest.

BELL POINT AREA

I consider the Bell Point area to be the part of the island extending from Goat Mountain (officially known as First Stick Hill) to the tip of Bell Point as well as the valley leading out to Bell Beach. On the eastern side, smaller hills lead up to the edge of Anse Marcel.

The southwest portion of this area includes the edge of Grand Case, but aside from the lower portions of Goat Mountain the area is mostly uninhabited. The line of hills extending to the point is topped with secondary forest, and the majority of the area is scrubland used as pasture for goats and cattle. There is a long rocky beach on the western side and Bell Beach is a small sandy beach at the end of the valley. A rocky cliff face leads from Bell Beach to the tip of Bell Point.

Although it is neither the prettiest nor most pristine area of the island, it is an excellent example of the hilly regions of the island, with some habitation at the lower elevations and mixed areas of pasture. Outside the towns and coastal resort areas, much of the island exists in a similarly degraded state.

On the hills it is interesting to note the relative defoliation due to grazing. In the areas with the densest goat populations, the ground is almost bare and rains wash significant amounts of soil into the sea. Areas grazed by cattle tend to contain more vegetation. While occasional goats may be seen in the hilltop forest, they seem to have less impact there. Cattle apparently lack either the ability or the desire to enter those areas.

In Bell Valley, the mongoose is quite common. As a result, the ground lizard *Amieva* is totally absent. This is also where I found the raccoon carcass. The presence of raccoons may also contribute to the lack of *Amieva* in this area.

Seaside cliffs ring the area from Bell Beach to the tip of Bell Point.

A small herd of goats surveys the landscape from the rocky outcrop at the tip of Bell Point.

During the late winter and early spring dry season much of the groundcover dies and some trees shed their leaves to conserve moisture.

Near the tip of Bell Point, a large grassy area divided by old stone walls overlooks the long rocky beach.

By summer, increased rainfall has enriched both the forest and the scrubland.

A view from Bell Beach towards Bell Point looks quite pretty. Just off the beach to the left is a large area of mud where pigs wallow.

The sedimentary rocks in the foreground jut up at the same angle as the exposed rock in the hillside behind them. Originally a volcanic island, St. Martin was submerged, capped with limestone and then thrust up again.

WILDERNESS

Wilderness is the largest undeveloped portion of the island, covering the northeastern point between Cul de Sac and Anse Marcel. A trail, which unfortunately begins at a landfill and ends at a sewage treatment plant, leads around this area, mostly near the shore. The small beach nestled in the middle, Petite Cayes, is probably the only place where you can swim out into the sea and look back on the island without seeing any evidence of humans.

The area includes long rocky beaches, a nice chunk of forest and a unique area of seaside vegetation that includes several varieties of cactus and a large variety of groundcover plants. Small signs along the trail identify many of the species found here.

The *Amieva* is quite rare in this area, probably due to the presence of mongoose. On the rocky shoreline, composed primarily of dead coral skeletons, *Anolis gingivinus* seems to occupy their niche.

The shoreline is an excellent place to see seabirds, particularly the magnificent frigatebird, perhaps because the area is exposed to the prevailing easterly winds.

The forested area along the trail between Petite Cayes and Anse Marcel is a bit different from the forests in the central mountains. Although it can be dense the trees are neither as tall nor as varied. This is likely due to the lower elevation and correspondingly less rainfall. One can't help but wonder how much of the island would be like this if it hadn't been cleared for agriculture.

Red Rock, the peak in the center of this area is forested up its entire slope on the sea-facing side, making it rather unique in that respect. On the island side, pasture stretches up to near the top as it does on so many hills.

The view of Petite Cayes and the mountains behind it is almost totally devoid of human development, making it a very important habitat for local wildlife.

The barrel cactus *Melocactus intortus* is quite common near the windblown Eastern Point of Wilderness. It is also referred to as the pope cactus or Turk's head cactus.

Much of the coastline at Wilderness is composed of dead coral skeletons from a variety of species washed up from the surrounding reefs.

Eastern Point juts out into the waters of the Atlantic Ocean. A variety of low groundcover gives way to wave-battered rocks near the shore.

The town of Colombier lies nestled at the foot of the central mountains. As can clearly be seen, this area is the most verdant part of the island.

CENTRAL MOUNTAINS

A series of mountains runs more or less north-to-south through the center of the island. The tallest, Pic Paradis is a little over 400 meters tall. These central mountains are connected by a series of trails that runs along the length of the crest.

While not tall enough to support a cloud forest, the upper altitudes of the central mountains are quite densely forested and support various bromeliads and other epiphytes. At least most of the original forest was cleared during colonial times. It is possible that some areas of the original forest survived, but the remnants of stone walls are often found even in the highest forests.

Numerous dry gulches run down the mountainsides offering natural paths to the peaks. During heavy rains these fill with water, and some small puddles may remain in rock cavities at least temporarily.

The forests of the central mountains are the primary habitat for a variety of organisms including helicinid snails, certain orb-weaving spiders and a variety of insects. The anole *Anolis pogus* and the two species of dwarf gecko are also common in these forests.

The forest may be referred to as semi-evergreen seasonal forest as a minority of trees do lose their leaves during the dry season. This type of forest is also called tropical dry forest, distinguishing it from rainforest or cloud forest. Although they receive less attention, tropical dry forests can have a level of diversity approaching that of rainforests. In some ways they are at more risk than rainforests, as only a minute fraction are currently protected and they are easily cleared for agriculture.

Hopefully this area will remain relatively undeveloped in the future. In addition to their environmental value, these mountains offer a scenic beauty that significantly enriches the island.

Despite the rapid pace of development on the island, the central mountains still contain large areas of undeveloped tropical dry forest.

Dense forests are home to a variety of plant and animal life, at times approaching the level of biodiversity present in rainforests.

Dry gulches, typically filled with boulders, are often the easiest route through mountain forests that can be quite dense.

Mountain clearings are a reminder of the colonial deforestation that stripped the forests from the majority of the Lesser Antilles.

Limestone outcrops are commonly found near the peaks of the central mountains.

Mangroves ring the small pond near the Grand Case cemetery. Many species not necessarily associated with wetlands are often found here, including the yellow warbler, which is particularly fond of the border between mangrove and scrubland.

MANGROVES AND SALT PONDS

Salt ponds and mangrove woodlands are an important ecosystem for many creatures, from birds to fish to invertebrates. They trap nutrients that would otherwise allow algae to overgrow coral reefs while serving as a nursery to many fish species that live there. They counteract coastal erosion and soften the blow of hurricanes.

On St. Martin there are over 20 salt ponds, most of which are surrounded by mangroves, as is a good portion of the large lagoon. The salt ponds are typically connected to the sea either permanently or seasonally. Of course, many wetland areas have been reclaimed (or more accurately, simply claimed) by man. Those that remain are typically highly polluted, but still support a variety of life.

Mangrove woodlands on the island are variously comprised of red mangrove (*Rhizophora mangle*), black mangrove (*Avicennia germinans*), white mangrove (*Laguncularia racemosa*) and buttonwood (*Conocarpus erecta*), as well as a variety of other plants that are adapted to saline environments.

Species highly dependent upon mangroves and salt pond include the majority of wading birds and waterfowl, iguanas, tropical fish of many varieties and many different invertebrates from crabs to the mangrove buckeye.

While two of the larger salt ponds on the French side and their mangrove woodlands are protected from development as part of the nature reserve, that protection does not include protection against, or the cleanup of, human waste flowing into them. More ominously, large areas of mangrove woodland bordering the lagoon on the Dutch side are being developed by new resorts and an expansion of the airport.

Roosting cattle egrets are a common site in salt pond mangroves, while many other species roost less conspicuously.

Beneath the surface of the water, mangroves provide a crucial habitat for juvenile fish and crustaceans as well as unique species like the mangrove upside-down jellyfish.

A large wetland area surrounding Salines d'Orient and Étang aux Poissons on the French side is under a certain degree of protection as part of the nature reserve.

The majority of salt ponds are at least seasonally connected to the surrounding sea. This is primarily done to avoid flooding during hurricanes or other heavy storms.

In some areas the vegetation surrounding salt ponds can be quite sparse, in this case resembling the American southwest perhaps more than a tropical island.

Cattle drink at a freshwater pond in the Bell Hill area. Man made ponds created for livestock are some of the largest and most important habitats for freshwater organisms.

FRESHWATER HABITATS

Fresh water is hard to find on Saint Martin. In the land of salt ponds, there are no rivers or freshwater lakes. Instead, there are small ponds, roadside ditches, puddles, wells and abandoned swimming pools. Despite the limited amount of fresh water available on the island, it is highly exploited by the wildlife.

The guppy (*Poecilia reticulata*), is referred to on the island as the millions because they are so common. With the added advantage of being able to live in brackish water in the salt ponds, they manage to colonize quickly wherever freshwater bodies occur, even temporarily.

Other typical freshwater organisms include many types of insects, including diving beetles, backswimmers, water striders and the larvae of mosquitoes, dragonflies and damselflies. Several types of freshwater snails are present on the island and may easily be found in road-side ditches. Tadpoles are common in almost any still fresh water on the island, but are less common in running water, where eggs and tadpoles may be eaten by guppies.

Many water sources are anthropogenic, at least in part. Some roadside ditches would be dry without sewage overflow or leaky water mains. The majority of ponds were created to provide water for livestock. Abandoned pools, or even barrels may provide habitat for freshwater organisms.

During the drier months, many freshwater sources may shrink or dry up entirely, making the freshwater lifestyle somewhat dangerous. However, when the rains return these ecosystems come back to life.

Guppies and aquatic snails are found in many freshwater bodies. Guppies are also able to tolerate salt water, allowing them to colonize any areas where running water is even temporarily connected to a salt pond.

The temporary nature of many freshwater bodies on the island can spell doom for unlucky guppies. These were found in an area where a temporary roadside ditch dried up.

A typical roadside ditch in Hope Estate. Depending on rainfall, it may be a continuous stream, or a collection of separate puddles.

Herons, egrets and other wading birds are often seen hunting for tadpoles and guppies in freshwater ponds like this one at the edge of a pasture.

The hot tub at the abandoned La Belle Creole resort serves as a home for two-striped treefrog tadpoles, as well as some guppies, although I have no idea how they got there.

The entrance to the larger chamber of La Grotte du Puits de Terres Basses. The large fan of debris upon which Yann and Marie are standing is probably a remnant of past mining.

BAT CAVES

There are currently two caves on the island known to be significant roosting and breeding areas for bats. The smaller cave is located in the cliffs at the top of Billy Folly above the Pelican in Simpson Bay. It can be accessed by taking the road past the Pelican, and a left on Pearl Drive, where you can park at the end of the street. The limestone cliff where the cave is located can be found above a large white villa which bears the improbable name Cleavage. The cave has two openings, a small hole at the top of Billy Folly with a tree growing out of it, and a slightly larger opening at the base of the cave through which you may crawl.

The main chamber is fairly large, perhaps ten meters in diameter and eight meters tall. A small number of bats may be seen roosting on the ceiling of this chamber and occasionally circling the cave. There are also a number of small chambers and holes in the sides of the cave, some of which are large enough for a human to enter.

The larger bat cave is located in the Terres Basses region of the island off Rue Rousseau, near a salt pond called Grand Étang. From the eastern edge of the pond, take approximately 300 paces down Rue Rousseau to the east and head up the hill to your left. Perhaps 100 meters into the forest and up the hill you will find La Grotte du Puits de Terres Basses (roughly translated as the cave of the well of the lowlands).

This cave has two large chambers with adjacent openings that are quite large, several meters across and easily tall enough to walk through. The caves are less enclosed than the Billy Folly cave, but much larger and are home to hundreds of bats. The floor of the larger left chamber is covered with the almond seeds and fruit pits, presumably discarded by bats. Cylindrical holes in the ceiling, possibly from previous phosphate mining, host dozens of bats, while in other areas, roosting bats blanket large areas of the ceiling. Multiple species can clearly be seen in this cave, often roosting in mixed aggregations. What I believe to be mothers surrounded by their young are also present.

It goes without saying that a visit to the bat caves (despite the stench, mosquitoes and overwhelming eeriness) is one of the most unique and thrilling natural adventures the island has to offer. I truly hope these natural wonders are preserved. Devil's Hole, the third and largest known bat cave on the island, was filled in during the 1990s.

Several openings in the eastern chamber of La Grotte de Puits allow a fair amount of light into the cave.

A small hole in the ceiling of the Billy Folly cave may be seen from the top of the hill.

The interior of the main chamber of the Billy Folly bat cave. Sunlight enters through a relatively small hole in the ceiling of the cave.

Bats in the eastern chamber are concentrated primarily on the ceiling of the darker areas of the cave.

The three islands in this photo are, from left to right, Tintamarre, Pinel and Little Key. All are essentially uninhabited, although Pinel has several businesses operating with the permission of the nature reserve and a residence built before the reserve was established.

TINTAMARRE AND PINEL

Tintamarre and Pinel are two satellite islands off the French side that are part of the nature reserve. Both are relatively flat and covered primarily with scrubland, although small patches of woodland and thickets are present. While Pinel is quite near shore and serviced by regular ferries, Tintamarre is somewhat less accessible, though still regularly visited. The traditional local name for Tintamarre is Flat Island.

Due to their isolation, the Lesser Antilles as a whole are home to many unique terrestrial species. The reptiles in particular are often studied as an example of adaptive radiation. Likewise, the satellite islands in the Lesser Antilles are similarly interesting. Although Tintamarre and Pinel are not known to harbor any endemic species as is the case for several other satellite islands in the Caribbean, differences in their fauna from that of St. Martin are of interest.

In the case of Tintamarre and Pinel, one interesting difference is the presence on Tintamarre of a separate subspecies of *Amieva plei* from the St. Martin population (*A. plei plei* on Tintamarre and *A. plei analifera* on St. Martin). On Pinel, *Amieva* seems to be absent entirely.

Satellite islands often fill an important role as the last refuge of endemic species that have become extinct on the main island. Typically this happens when introduced pests, such as the mongoose, are present on the main island but not the satellite. I believe it is possible that *Iguana delicatissima*, which seems to be completely extinct on St. Martin, may survive on Tintamarre.

Unfortunately, invasive species are not unknown on these satellites. Rats are present on Pinel and Tintamarre, and Tintamarre also has wild goats. Still, with their protected status and relative isolation, these two islets may play an important role in the preservation of St. Martin's wildlife.

Dense thickets are present in small areas of Pinel, offering habitat for animals like the dwarf geckos, which are typically found in the mountain forests.

Pinel sports a variety of coastal vegetation surrounding an interior comprised mostly of scrubland.

The scrubland that dominates Pinel and Tintamarre closely resembles that of St. Martin.

Tintamarre as seen from Wilderness. Both islands are quite flat and lack any significant source of fresh water.

Brown boobies roost on a rock outcrop near the beach on Tintamarre, where they have for years. (Photo by M.P.)

Tintamarre's coastline features rocky cliffs that are popular nesting sites for various seabirds as well as sandy beaches.

SPECIAL THANKS AND CREDITS

I'd like to thank a whole bunch of people for their help in producing this book, both direct and indirect:

Jennifer Yerkes, Yann del Barco, Marie Amiguet, Stephen Winkel & Olivia Roudon, Emile Lake, Alain, Marc & Kristin Petrelluzzi, Chris and Sally Davies, Stuart Bennett, Aurelien Roger, Chris and Theresa Luty, Tom Turner, Mark de Silva, Father Sanchez, Jo-Anne Sewlal, Barbara Cannegieter, Fons O'Connor, Elsje Bosch, the entire Les Fruits de Mer team, Calmos Cafe, Octopus Diving and the Sint Maarten Museum.

All photos are by Mark Yokoyama, except as noted. M.P. is Marc Petrelluzzi, M.A. is Marie Amiguet. The back cover photo of the author is by Jennifer Yerkes.

ADDITIONAL READING

I have a few recommendations for anyone interested in Caribbean wildlife. *Reptiles and Amphibians of the Eastern Caribbean* by Anita Malhotra and Roger S. Thompson is an excellent overview with summaries for each of the Lesser Antilles. *Birds of the West Indies* from Princeton Field Guides is superb, including all species recorded in the region. *Studies on the Fauna of Curaçao and Other Caribbean Islands* is two large bookshelves worth of scientific research going back to the 1940s, and is available in the reading room at the Sint Maarten Museum. *Biological Inventory of Sint Maarten* by Anna Rojer is an excellent overview and you can find the article online.

Made in the USA
Charleston, SC
29 July 2012